CHILDREN WITH SPECIAL NEEDS

ABOUT THE AUTHOR

Karen Lungu earned her bachelor's degree from Dallas Christian College. During this time she served in two internships: on the Navajo Indian Reservation, and in South Korea, where she worked in a leper village and in various orphanages with differently-abled children.

Mrs. Lungu received a masters degree in education, guidance and counseling from the University of Colorado. She completed her field work with Sangre De Cristo Hospice and as a therapist in family and marriage counseling.

She and her husband have adopted six children and have two birthchildren. She offers training in adoption issues and in raising children with special needs.

Today, she and her husband live in Colorado with their seven children. They continue to operate a therapuetic foster home and a temporary receiving home for children with special needs.

CHILDREN
WITH
SPECIAL NEEDS

*A Resource Guide for Parents, Educators,
Social Workers, and Other Caregivers*

By

KAREN L. LUNGU, M.A.

Foreword by

Linda Olds, M.A.

CHARLES C THOMAS • PUBLISHER, LTD.
Springfield • Illinois • U.S.A.

Published and Distributed Throughout the World by

CHARLES C THOMAS • PUBLISHER, LTD.
2600 South First Street
Springfield, Illinois 62794-9265

© *1999 by* CHARLES C THOMAS • PUBLISHER, LTD.
ISBN 0-398-06933-6 (cloth)
ISBN 0-398-06934-4 (paper)

Library of Congress Catalog Card Number: 98-47290

With THOMAS BOOKS *careful attention is given to all details of manufacturing
and design. It is the Publisher's desire to present books that are satisfactory as to their
physical qualities and artistic possibilities and appropriate for their particular use.*
THOMAS BOOKS *will be true to those laws of quality that assure a good name
and good will.*

Printed in the United States of America
CR-R-3

Library of Congress Cataloging in Publication Data

Lungu, Karen L.
    Children with special needs : a resource guide for parents,
educators, social workers, and other caregivers / by Karen L. Lungu
; foreword by Linda Olds.
        p.   cm.
    Includes bibliographical references and index.
    ISBN 0-398-06933-6 (cloth). -- ISBN 0-398-06934-4 (pbk.)
    1. Handicapped children--Care--United States. 2. Developmentally
disabled children--Care--United States. 3. Children of prenatal alcohol
abuse--Care--United States. 4. Infants (Premature)--Care--United States.
5. Handicapped children--Services for--United States. 6. Developmentally
disabled children--Services for--United States. 7. Children of prenatal
alcohol abuse--Services for --United Sates. 8. Infants (Premature)--Services
for--United States. 9. Special needs adoption--United States. I. Title.
HV1553.L86   1999
362.7'0973--dc21   98-47290
                                                                          CIP

FOREWORD

When Karen Lungu first approached me with her idea for writing *CHILDREN WITH SPECIAL NEEDS*, I was intrigued. Now in its completion, I am convinced. This book is an excellent resource in providing expertise and insight on differently-abled children. A large and diverse audience will benefit from this book.

Being a special and regular elementary educator for the past twenty years, I have taught in the full range of educational settings with children who have special needs. Many models are available for teaching differently-abled children. They include special schools, different types of classrooms, or full inclusion, where children with special needs are educated in regular classrooms alongside their same-aged peers. These models continue to change as more is learned about the increasing population of children with special needs. A child's individual mental, social, emotional, and physical needs must be heavily considered in finding the best educational placement. This book provides a wealth of diligently researched information to assist all caregivers in making these decisions in raising and educating all children with special needs.

Children With Special Needs is an invaluable tool in providing a unique perspective of family life to seasoned educators and newcomers in the field. I have spent many hours listening to parents share their dreams and challenges in raising their children. Mrs. Lungu offers a book with a personal and professional point of view which will serve other parents, educators, and caregivers of children with special needs. From an educatorís angle, this is a book which goes beyond the classroom walls and provides those of us in the teaching profession a unique insight that no other resource has yet to provide. We thank you, Mrs. Lungu, for sharing your experience and that of your family.

LINDA OLDS, M.A.

PREFACE

There are many good books on the market dealing with specific special challenges faced by children today. However, medically fragile children with more complex conditions are leaving the hospitals earlier than ever. It is not necessarily that there is an increase of children with special needs, but with medical advances, more are surviving. Also, treatment of children with special needs has changed. For example, years ago, a child with intellectual disabilities and severe heart complications may not have been as aggressively treated as today. With fertility treatment advances, there are more multiple births as well, resulting in an increase of infants and children with a number of special challenges.

As an adoptive and foster parent, I have seen the trends change as well. We are seeing more children with multiple disabilities due to drug or alcohol exposure, and more children with significant attachment issues. Though quite a bit of research has been done on children who have been prenatally exposed to alcohol, the studies on children who have been exposed to drugs in utero is still inconclusive. And, although there are differing opinions on how to handle children with attachment issues, those parents who have tried to rear an unattached child know there are no exact formulas or answers. Often it depends on a combination of temperament, personality, social history, and family environment.

All of these and the ever changing policies regarding insurance and managed health care mean that more parents are becoming the primary, health, medical, and educational caretakers of children with special challenges. More parents are learning complex medical procedures in order to care for their children at home. And, we parents and other caregivers of children with special needs are learning more techniques in occupational and physical therapy, speech pathology, diet, and education. My husband and I have often found that a child or foster child of ours qualifies for only three months of therapy when we are convinced he or she needs much more than that. We have watched the parade of vision specialists, speech therapists, home health care nurses, respiratory therapists, hospice workers, social workers, and countless others in our home. Ultimately, we, as parents, have had to learn their techniques when the 30-minute session is over. This book picks up where that type of support leaves off.

Those parents who are raising children with special needs understand that their homes are forever changed. They have become well versed in medical technology; they spend a great amount of time in IEP staffings; they study the laws which affect the rights and education of their children.

We have come to understand that our children may not be considered typical, but we will do everything to advocate for their best interest.

I remember a morning when my husband and I were ushered out of our daughter's hospital room just before a medical procedure. One of the healthcare professionals admonished, "parents just don't need to see everything." Years later, we chose to stay by my son's bedside as the neurologist performed a series of tests to determine his brain function. I have come to believe, from the parents who have found themselves in similar situations, that many of us believe the same things: we want to understand; we want to know the definition of each   and every medical term; we need to know what to expect; we strive to learn how to advocate for the best interest of our children; and we want to know how to help the educators and other caregivers who work with our children and the special challenges they face.

My purpose in writing this book is to help other parents of differently-abled children to find the resources needed to raise, educate, and advocate for their families and all the challenges their differently-abled child faces. I have tried to cover many of the developmental disabilities faced by families today. I have also placed a great deal of emphasis on the special needs of adoptive and foster families. I hope this book is helpful in directing parents, educators and other caregivers to the resources, support groups, national organizations and other avenues of advocacy to best support the child with special needs.

K.L.L.

INTRODUCTION

DAVID'S STORY

My husband Ron and I are on numerous mailing lists concerned with adoption issues and we subscribe to several exchanges whose primary focus is to place children with special needs. One of these is *The CAP Book*, Children Awaiting Parents. *The CAP Book* is a national directory of waiting children, published by Children Awaiting Parents, Inc. Currently, it registers over 400 waiting children. It was through *The CAP Book* that we first learned of our son, David. We received one of our bimonthly updates of waiting children in September, 1994. Often, when caseworkers and agencies have been unable to place children locally, they register them with a national directory such as CAP for possible recruitment of adoptive parents. David's picture and write-up caught our attention immediately. His brief biography read as follows:

> **David**, black, 2 years old, born September 1992, is a happy, personable toddler who always has a smile. He is developmentally delayed but is making progress in his foster home. David loves Barney, Sesame Street and stuffed animals. He sits up, crawls, walks around furniture and babbles constantly. David is a medically needy child who has frequent doctor appointments and requires close monitoring. He has had successful heart surgery but continues to have respiratory and feeding needs. David needs a family who is willing to learn about his special needs and give him lots of individual attention. The agency will consider all families interested in David.

We were very interested in David and began the process of determining if we could be considered as a possible placement for him. We contacted CAP which gave us the name and number of David's caseworker. The caseworker gave us a few more details on David's medical history and encouraged us to send in our home study and other relevant family information. All through the holidays we waited for a response. We kept in touch with David's caseworker by phone through the months.

Because David was out of state and his medical needs were numerous, the agency continued to try to recruit adoptive parents closer to home. Finally, we received the call we had hoped for; we had been chosen as David's adoptive family. Our next step was to get through all the paperwork for Interstate Compact in order to bring our new son home. This process took another few weeks. In the meantime, we began to prepare for David's arrival. Because he was still on a heart monitor and required a feeding pump 21 hours a day, we decided he needed his own room. Our other six children had a lot of fun decorating and getting his room ready.

All through this period, we were receiving letters and calls from David's caseworker informing us as to what we would need before his arrival. The first checklist she sent us read as follows:

1. Identify a home health medical center
2. Need an aerosol machine and equipment to run it
3. Need heart monitor
4. Portable G-Tube, companion pump, and transporter
5. Pediatric cardiologist
6. Nursing pool for home health care hours

After both states agreed to the interstate compact and placement, I was finally able to fly out and spend some time with David. I will never forget my first look at my newest child. It was after 11:00 P.M. and he was in his crib but not asleep. Because of his severe reflux, he slept in a reflux sling with the crib mattress set several inches higher at the head. David was rocking himself back and forth in the sling when I walked into his room. I would later learn that he did this every time he was in his crib. It was a self-comforting behavior and may have been due to the severe neglect he experienced as an infant, and as a result of the prenatal crack cocaine exposure. As I peered in on him, David's eyes widened and he gave me an excited grin. With a pacifier still clenched between his teeth, his first word to me was "Yeah."

David captured my heart with one look. I spent a few days with him in his foster home. I learned how to operate his feeding pump and other monitors, how to give him his medications and nebulizer treatments, and how to follow his schedule. I also met some of his therapists. I found it difficult to leave David when it was time to fly home; he was already as dear to me as my other children.

We spent the next week getting all of David's medical equipment set up before his arrival. David's foster parents flew him in a week after my visit. Our other children were so excited they set up chairs by the front door hours ahead of his scheduled arrival. The children and Ron fell in love with David immediately, just as I had. He was a special child who had a knack for charming people everywhere he went. After a brief visit that first evening, the foster parents left and we began settling David into his new family. We worked on getting into a routine that first week, trying to keep as close to the schedule David had been used to in the foster home. His breathing treatments were numerous and we had to learn to maneuver his feeding pump, but we never wavered in our decision; David was our son. Our older children were good about sitting with him while he watched his favorite Barney movie every morning. His activities were limited, but he never seemed to mind. David stayed up in the evenings after the other children were in bed so that Ron and I could have special time with him.

Soon we were planning for Easter. It was exciting to think about our first holiday with our new son. On the Friday before Easter, I noticed that David seemed to be breathing heavier and he appeared to be fighting a cold. I had just taken him in to see the pediatrician two days prior, so he was already on antibiotics. I called the doctor again and was told to increase his breathing treatments and see how the weekend went. The next evening David stayed up as I filled plastic eggs and arranged baskets. He didn't act as he usually did during our evening times together. He didn't want to play and he seemed tired. He kept putting his head on Ron's shoulder and Ron commented how David didn't seem himself.

We had a fairly quiet Easter. David walked around out front with his new Easter basket while the other children collected eggs. They all put a few in his basket but he seemed content to just watch the activity. He took a long afternoon nap, but he continued to act lethargic and my worry grew. He put his head on my shoulder as I gave him his breathing treatments that evening and into the night. The next morning, I called the pediatrician's office to see about getting him in again. David seemed to have worsened. He was coughing a great deal and he appeared even more lethargic than before. As I waited for the office to call me back I put David down for his nap.

At 1:00 P.M., I began to give David another nebulizer treatment. Again, he put his head on my shoulder. All of a sudden, I heard a deep gasp and his body went stiff. His lips turned blue and his eyes rolled back. With David still in my arms I called 911 and the operator started talking me through rescue breathing as I waited for the ambulance; it arrived in just under two minutes. My neighbor ran over and took the other children to her home as the paramedics worked on David.

An officer took me to the hospital where David had been transported. I was met at the emergency entrance by a hospital chaplain who took me to a private room while the doctors and nurses continued to work on my son. It was a half hour later when someone came in to tell me they had been able to get David's heart started again, and they would be transferring him to Children's Hospital. I rode in the ambulance with David this time. I remember thinking it was a miracle and now that his heart was working again, he would be fine.

That evening Ron and I met with David's medical team. We were told that although David's CAT scan looked good, it would be a few days before we would all be able to determine the extent of his recovery. One nurse pulled me aside and told me I needed to understand that David may have suffered irreversible brain damage from the lack of oxygen and it was possible he may never wake up.

I spent day and night by David's bedside for the next few days. His body became stiffer, which was not a good sign. I was told it was an indication of the extent of brain damage he suffered. It was called posturing and it meant his brain had no control over his movements. He remained on a respirator and he was suctioned often. The morning of his scheduled neurological exam was April 19, 1995. The television was on in David's room and nurses had gathered as we watched in horror the news of the bombing of the Alfred P. Murrah Building in Oklahoma City. That morning, I remember understanding the fear of parents who waited to see if their children survived.

As the television continued its uninterrupted coverage of the tragedy, three physicians began the exam. They warned me that it would look brutal. I watched as they filled a large syringe with ice water. They injected it into each ear and watched for any response from his pupils. They prodded and tapped and looked for any type of reflex. Their faces remained grim and they confirmed our worst fears, David's coma was irreversible. He had only minimal brainstem activity and no higher cortical functioning. We were told the respirator was the only thing keeping David alive. It was explained that he would probably breathe on his own for a while if he were taken off the respirator, but since he had no gag or cough, he would not be able to keep his airways open. Another physician and caseworker came in to encourage us to bring in the older children to say good-bye to their brother. None of the children had seen David since the day he was taken so abruptly from our home.

However, things became more complicated since we had not yet finalized David's adoption. We could not give the decision to turn off the life support machines at the time. The agency which had placed David was unsure as to how to pursue the matter. We waited for nearly two weeks without hearing from them. They finally informed us they would not give permission to terminate life-support. They told us we could either cancel the placement and they would place David into a full-care facility, or we could finalize the adoption and make our own decisions concerning David's medical care.

For us it was never a question, David was our son and we wanted to finalize the placement. We were able to get into court the next week and the same judge who had finalized two of our other placements heard our family's story. He granted the petition to adopt immediately.

That evening, a friend came over to watch the other children while Ron and I went to the hospital to be with David as his respirator was turned off. The nurses had moved David to a private corner room of the ICU and placed a rocking chair by his bed. They had made stamped imprints of his hand and foot on cards for us to keep. A doctor came in to describe how David's last minutes or hours would go and what to expect. Someone had dressed David in one of his favorite sleepers. The respirator tube was removed around 7:30 P.M. Ron and I took turns holding our son as we listened to his labored breathing, fearing that last breath. We had been told that he would probably stop breathing within one to three hours. However, David continued to breathe into the night and all through the next day. We talked to the hospital staff about taking him home and giving his brothers and sisters a chance to hold him before he died.

Once home, we settled David on the couch surrounded by his favorite stuffed animals and blankets. We put his Barney tape on and played it over and over for him. Our pediatrician's office contacted hospice. They came out the next day to help our family with David's last days. David continued to breathe through the week. We had time to hold him, sing to him, and accept that our son was going to die. We needed that time as a family and I was grateful we were able to bring David home. David died quietly on a rainy Sunday morning that May.

This book is lovingly dedicated to the very dear and cherished memory of my son, David Michael Lungu.

ACKNOWLEDGMENTS

Iwould like to thank the following people: My husband Ron, who always gives great support and encouragement; my dear friend Linda Olds for all of her support help and suggestions; my friends at Cherry Drive Elementary; Diane Strevey and Dr. Barb Shedore for their contributions; our friends at Good Shepherd United Methodist Church, especially my UMW group and my favorite preschool teachers—all who helped our family through so many additions and a very difficult period; the ICU staff at Denver Children's Hospital; hospital Chaplain, Reverend Jane L. Keener; Peggy, Linda, and Paula of St. John's Hospice; all of our friends and neighbors who provided meals, baby-sitting, and transportation during David's illness; a very special thank you to dear friends Lynette and Eric Hixson, Reverend Bob and Gin Link, Lisa and Eric Miller, and Kim and Steve Easterday-McPadden; Peggy Soule, Executive Director of Children Awaiting Parents, Inc.; Lynda Cicero and Linda Nelson, our first caseworkers; our new friends at Deer Park United Methodist Church, with a special thanks to Dave for the computer help; and, a warm hug to my children, Cody, Kelsey, Taylor, Nathan, McKinsey, Matthew, and Grady—I love you all.

CONTENTS

CHILDREN WITH SPECIAL NEEDS

Chapter 1

PRENATAL DRUG AND ALCOHOL EXPOSURE

MORE ABOUT DAVID

The brief introduction we read about David in *The CAP Book* didn't even begin to cover our son's story. After David's placement, we received a copy of his "Child Study Inventory." In part, this study read: "David was born on September 25, 1992 at 5:47 A.M. He was born premature at 33 weeks gestation, weighing only 4 lb., 3 oz. At three days of age, David received a cardiac catherization. David also had transposition of the great arteries. David has a history of medical problems and continues to. He has bronciopulmonary dysplasia, gastroesophagus, reflux, a g-tube, and reactive airway disease, among other diagnoses. David has a lot of medical needs. He has D-transposition of the great vessels, for which he had surgery. He will require additional surgery to finish correcting this problem. David is on several medications and he will probably have to continue these for awhile. He is currently on constant g-tube feeding and unable to take any foods by mouth. David was born exposed to crack cocaine. At birth, both mother and David tested positive for cocaine and other drugs. The birth mother admitted to using crack and drinking during pregnancy."

FETAL ALCOHOL SYNDROME

Many of the waiting children and infants in special needs adoption programs have been affected by drugs, alcohol, or both in utero. Some agencies no longer list drug or alcohol exposure as a "special need" in their infant programs because all of their babies have been drug or alcohol exposed to a certain extent. Today, fetal alcohol syndrome is the number one cause of mental retardation in our country. Children with fetal alcohol effects are more likely to have normal IQs, but they experience many of the same behaviors and learning disabilities as FAS children. At this time, one in every 500 to 700 babies born in the United States is a fetal alcohol syndrome baby. One in 300 to 350 has fetal alcohol effects.

Fetal alcohol syndrome is characterized by one or more of the following: the infant or child being small-for-gestational age; droopy eyelids; microcephaly; a flat midface and nasal bridge; the absence of a ridge between the nose and the upper lip; the forehead may protrude and the chin may be pointed; joint abnormalities; mild to moderate mental retardation due to damage of the central nervous system; congenital heart disease. Infants with this syndrome are often extremely irritable and inconsolable. Frequently they are hyperactive throughout childhood and as adults.

When a pregnant woman consumes alcohol, it breaks down to form acetaldehyde which is an extremely toxic substance. It is when this substance interacts with embryonic tissue on a continuing basis throughout a pregnancy that the syndrome can occur. The extent of malformation and abnormalities depends largely on the amount of alcohol consumed, whether the drinking was in binges, and at what point during the pregnancy the alcohol was ingested. In general, a woman taking two drinks a day throughout the pregnancy will have a small infant. Women having 4 to 6 drinks a day will often have babies who experience fetal alcohol effects. Eight to 10 drinks a day can have the result of fetal alcohol syndrome.

FETAL ALCOHOL EFFECTS

Infants and children diagnosed with fetal alcohol effects are challenged to a somewhat lesser degree. They do not have the facial features found in FAS, and so they may look perfectly normal. Although many of these children are preterm and subsequently developmentally delayed during infancy, they are often on target by the age of three. However, many of their special needs do not show up until they are school age. FAE children often struggle with ADHD (attention deficit with hyperactivity disorder), ADD (attention deficit disorder), or auditory/perceptual disorder. These children usually exhibit extremely poor judgment and have trouble connecting consequences and actions. This will often result in poor school performance. With early intervention, children, parents, and educators can learn ways to compensate for the disabilities. Speech and language professionals can help these children to become more visual learners, since the connection between what they hear and what they perceive is often scattered.

DEVELOPMENTAL STAGES OF FAS/FAE CHILDREN

Infants affected by either FAS of FAE may show one or more of the following: May have tremors and have the smell of alcohol at birth; very irritable; poor sucking ability; intolerant to stimulation, including being held; are slow to develop. Toddlers and preschoolers may exhibit the following: may be hyperactive or appear lethargic; need constant supervision because they do not comprehend boundaries and do not connect actions and consequences; are very physically demonstrative and demand attention; have a lack of fear which puts them at higher risks for accidents; or exhibit poor memory. FAS and FAE children of grade school age may demonstrate the following characteristics: continue to require much one-on-one attention; have difficulty staying on task; are very easily distracted and tend to distract others; have poor coordination; demonstrate extremely poor judgment; may read and write, but have difficulty learning both and remembering what has been learned; have fewer social skills; may exhibit intolerance or frustration through temper tantrums, crying often; or inappropriate handling of anger.

Reaching junior high, FAS and FAE children may show problems in the following areas: extreme difficulty keeping up academically and socially which will manifest itself in low self-esteem and rejection by peers and this may then lead them into the cycle of negative behaviors to get any type of attention and recognition, such as stealing, cheating, lying, fighting, etc.; continue to have poor judgment and inability to connect actions and consequences; continue to exhibit a lack of fear.

At high school age, FAS/FAE children tend to have problems in the following areas: continue to get into trouble, and/or continue cycle of being a victim; impulse control is very poor; little concept of how to handle money; in extreme cases of FAS basic living skills and hygiene care need to be retaught daily; continue to require much supervision.

The damage of FAS/FAE is not curable, and cannot be outgrown. There is more hope for the FAE child to learn different coping skills and compensation for the impairments than the FAS child. The FAS child will probably require a caretaker even into adulthood.

CRACK COCAINE AND DRUG EXPOSURE

The drug of choice today, and the one in which prospective adoptive parents of special needs children will most likely have to consider, is crack cocaine. Studies of the long-term effects of crack cocaine exposure are very limited because crack has not been around long enough for extensive research of how children are affected late in adolescence and into adulthood. Crack cocaine appeared on the scene in the mid-1980s. It is less expensive than other methamphetamines and extremely addictive.

We do know that crack can be devastating for infants in utero and well after birth. During pregnancy crack cocaine can cause deformities even to already perfectly formed organs by interfering with the blood flow to the fetus. This is especially true of the brain. About 35 percent of crack-exposed infants will have some type of cranial abnormality. Much of this damage is centered around the frontal lobes and basal ganglia, the effects of which show up in visual motor and social tasks. This is also why many crack-exposed children have some type of seizure disorder. In addition, delayed athetoid cerebral palsy may occur.

LONG-TERM EFFECTS AND PROGNOSIS

Like alcohol, crack exposure will generally result in a preterm infant which increases the likelihood of numerous medical challenges from birth. Many crack-exposed infants are unable to keep food down due to reflux. They are prone to muscle spasms and trembling. They alternate between brief bouts of restless sleep and high-pitched screaming.

They resist cuddling and other human contact by arching their backs. This is also a signal of possible nervous system damage. The more severely affected infants have stiffening of the hands, a trancelike stare, and have difficulty with sucking, swallowing, and eating. By nine months of age, there is evidence of fine motor coordination difficulty. And, by two years of age, they exhibit speech articulation difficulties. Most drug exposed infants who are preterm have underdeveloped lungs which can result in respiratory problems for several years. Many of these children require daily breathing treatments and may have even longer-term challenges with asthma.

Preterm and medically fragile infants are generally developmentally delayed. If the drug exposure was relatively mild and they outgrow the medical challenges, it is possible for drug exposed infants to be on target developmentally by preschool age. However, preliminary studies have shown that many drug-exposed children have difficulty with concentration and learning. About 25 percent have developmental delays beyond school age and around 40 percent have the neurological impairments which can affect the areas of socializing and functioning within a school environment. Almost all have problems with adaptive behavior, fine motor and cognitive skill, and language, to a certain degree. These challenges will manifest themselves in many of the same problem areas FAE kids experience, such as the increased possibility of ADD and ADHD, and auditory perceptual disorder.

It will be several more decades before researchers can offer a more complete picture of the long-term effects of crack exposed infants; however, it is clear that these are children whose challenges are far reaching in so many areas. They are almost always medically fragile with an uphill battle the first few years of their lives. The General Accounting Office estimates that there are at least 400,000 drug-exposed infants born each year. The September 18, 1991 issue of the *Denver Rocky Mountain News* offers a study that found that $500 million was spent on hospital care for thousands of drug-exposed infants in New York City alone. Most of the infants entering foster care in New York City are crack or cocaine exposed. Because the street prices of these particular drugs have dropped, more teenagers are using them at an earlier age, resulting in an increase of drug-exposed babies.

Dr. Ira Chasnoff of NAPARE (National Association for Perinatal Addiction Research) is currently conducting a seven-year study, one of the longest-running research projects on cocaine-exposed infants. His group is following 300 cocaine-exposed infants from birth. They were entered into an intensive intervention program. At age three, 90 of the children were tested. Normal intelligence showed up in 90 percent; 70 percent showed no behavioral difficulties; and 60 percent did not require speech therapy. Dr. Chasnoff maintains that the environment of the drug-exposed child is of as equal importance as the biology. He goes on to assert that by addressing the stability of the home and discovering strategies which help the child learn to focus, parents can even raise the IQ of the cocaine-exposed child. This is especially encouraging news for the prospective adoptive parent considering the special needs of drug-exposed children.

In 1992, the Child Welfare League of America surveyed 72 hospitals in 12 cities and found a record 607 babies a month could not be discharged because the birth parents were unable or unwilling to take them home. An overwhelming 85 percent of the babies in the CWLA survey were exposed to drugs or alcohol in the womb. As this time, there are well over 400,000 children awaiting adoptive placements in the US. This is an increase of over 50 percent since 1986, the year crack cocaine appeared on the streets.

Those seriously considering adopting a child with special needs will undoubtedly be faced with some weighty decisions concerning drug and alcohol exposure. All of the areas of developmental disability caused by drug or alcohol exposure in utero are covered in greater detail throughout this book.

Chapter 2

PREMATURE BIRTH

GRADY'S STORY

Grady was born November 22, 1994 at an estimated 28 weeks to 30 weeks gestation. He weighed 1 lb., 15 oz. or just under 900 grams. His initial diagnoses read as follows:

Respiratory Distress Syndrome in Newborn
Neonatal Jaundice Associated with Preterm Delivery
Pulmonary Hemorrhage of Newborn/Fetus
Intraventricular Hemorrhage of Fetus or Newborn
Late Metabolic Acidosis of Newborn
750 - 999 Grams
Fetal Distress First Noted During Labor, in Liveborn Infant
Patent Ductus Arteriosus
Respiratory Problems after Birth
Anemia of Prematurity
Other Diseases of the Lung, Not Elsewhere Classified
Inguinal Hernia without Obstruction/Gangrene Esophageal Reflux
Retrolental Fibroplasia

Grady began receiving continuous ventilation for respiratory support and he required some transfusions of packed cells. He remained hospitalized for the next five months, at which time he was placed in foster care. He remained on oxygen and a heart monitor 24 hours a day. Because of his severe reflux, Grady was once again hospitalized in order to undergo surgery for a procedure called Nissan Fundiplication. This allowed Grady to take in foods without regurgitating them into his lungs. He also received a G-tube so that formula was given through a feeding pump directly through the stomach wall.

Grady was again placed in a therapeutic foster home until termina-
tion of parental rights. At age 18 months, he was placed with our family. At this time, he had just been introduced to solid foods, though the
GI tube remained in place as a precaution. His primary diagnosis was
Chronic Lung Disease due to prematurity. His secondary diagnosis
was Gastrosophageal Reflux, S/P Nissan Fundoplication. Because of
David's similar special challenges, we were already familiar with gas-
trostomy tube feedings and deep suctioning procedures.

As is so often the case with medically fragile infants, so much effort
is extended toward survival that typical developmental milestones are
missed or delayed. Children on GI tubes miss out on significant oral
stimulation which delays speech. At the time of adoptive placement,
Grady was delayed in fine and gross motor skills, expressive communication, and auditory communication. Grady's situation was further
complicated in that his prematurity was due to his birth mother's drug
and alcohol use during the pregnancy, although the exact amount of
prenatal exposure was undetermined.

CAUSES OF PREMATURE BIRTH

About 2 percent of all deliveries result in premature birth; however,
20 percent of adolescent pregnancies will end in premature birth. This
may be due to the immature uterus of the adolescent.

Another common cause of premature birth is placental abruptia.
This is when the placenta pulls away from the uterine wall. It can
cause painful uterine bleeding. It is often a result of high blood pressure and heavy smoking.

Placenta previa is the term used when the placenta covers the cer-
vical opening of the birth canal. Although it is generally painless, it can
cause considerable bleeding and be life-threatening to the baby and
the mother.

Toxemia is characterized protein in the urine, excess fluid retention,
and high blood pressure. There may also be rapid and considerable
weight gain, frequent headaches, and eye problems. If left untreated,
it will progress to eclampsia, which is a reduction of the blood flow
within the placenta. This can be life-threatening to the baby and mother. Women with a history of hypertension, diabetes, or kidney disease
are more likely to develop toxemia.

Another cause of premature birth are uterine fibroids. These are noncancerous growths within the wall of the uterus. Benign growths can lead to placental abruption or a slowing of growth for the fetus.

Ruptured membranes will lead to premature birth also. If the rupture occurs before the 34th week of gestation, the attending physicians will try to withhold delivery. However, there is a great risk of infection for the baby and the mother during this unprotected period. Should the mother develop a fever, the baby will be delivered immediately.

Polyhydramnios is the term used to describe the condition of having too much amniotic fluid in the uterine cavity. Ologohydramnios is the term used when there is too little amniotic fluid. This can seriously inhibit fetal growth. In addition to being a cause of premature birth, both conditions often lead to a variety of birth defects.

Multiple births are much more likely to lead to prematurity than single births. This is because of the extra stress placed on the uterus, which can also lead to placenta previa, placental abruption, premature rupture of the membranes, or polyhydramnios. And, as stated in the first chapter, premature birth is often the result of drug or alcohol exposure. This, too, is due to the decrease of blood flow to the fetus and the additional stress placed upon the baby. This can be related to insufficient prenatal care as well. Many of the complications associated with drug and alcohol exposure may go undetected without the benefit of early medical intervention. There is a difference between an infant who is small due to a premature birth, and those who are considered small-for-gestational age (SGA). Many drug-exposed infants are born prematurely. However, many FAS/FAE children are small-for-gestational age. SGA infants are those who are small in size for their gestational age. Grady and David were both preterm and considered SGA. Babies born SGA can be born preterm or full-term. Many have the same complications as the premature infant with the exception of respiratory distress syndrome. They do tend to be underweight throughout life, and they have a higher incidence of learning disabilities and attention deficit disorder. Preterm SGA infants are at an increased risk for mental retardation and cerebral palsy.

CHARACTERISTICS OF THE PRETERM INFANT

There are physical and neurological differences in   preterm infants which distinguish them from the full-term baby. Preterm infants have a reddish skin color; there is an absence of skin creases, ear cartilage, and breast buds; and they have fine hair, or lunugo, over the entire body. The skin is redder in color because the blood vessels are closer to the surface. Breast buds, and cartilage in the ear lobe usually appear around the 34th week of gestation. During the third trimester neurological development involves an increase in muscle tone and changes in the mobility of the joints and reflex activity. The preterm infant has little muscle tone while the full-term infant will lay in a more flexed position.

APGAR SCORES

When a newborn is one minute of age, the attending physician will give an apgar score based on how well the baby is adjusting to his or her new environment. The apgar rating system was developed by Dr. Virginia Apgar. Now her name is used as an acronym for the five areas evaluated.

A refers to appearance such as the skin color.

P refers to pulse rate.

G is for grimace, which is the baby's response to stimulation.

A applies to activity. This generally is related to the area of muscle tone in the infant's arms and legs.

R refers to respiration. This is rated by how well the infant breathes and cries on his own.

A combined APGAR score under seven is an indication that the baby is in some kind of distress. The same evaluation is given again at five and ten minutes of age which will help the medicat team to determine whether the baby is progressing or if his condition is deteriorating.

COMPLICATIONS OF PREMATURITY

In addition to the neurological and physical differences between full-term and preterm infants, there is an increased risk of complications during the newborn period of premature infants. These include respiratory distress syndrome, patent ductus artiosus, apnea, biochemical abnormalities, retrolental fibroplasia, and necrotizing enterocolitis.

Respiratory distress syndrome affects approximately 20 percent of all premature infants, more often those born before 32 weeks gestation. It is also referred to as hyaline membrane disease and it can develop within a few hours or a few days after birth. It is characterized by grunting respirations as the infant has to expend a great amount of energy to breathe. It is caused by an inability to produce a chemical substance in the infant's underdeveloped lungs. The infant will begin to use abdominal muscles to try and breathe because the lungs are not expanding properly. In a full-term infant, the first few breaths after birth will open the alveoli, or air pockets, of the lungs. The alveoli are coated with the chemical substance surfactant, which prevents the air pockets from closing. Surfactant begins to develop within the infant between 32 to around the 36th week of gestation. Premature infants often lack enough surfactant to keep the alveoli from collapsing.

The severity of the respiratory distress will determine the treatment needed. Some infants will only need supplemental oxygen by mask. If the distress is more severe, the infant may need an endotracheal tube placed in the trachea, or windpipe, to aid in breathing. This tube is connected to a respirator which takes over the breathing for the infant. Babies will usually begin to recover as their lungs mature.

Bronchopulmonary dysplasia is a condition associated with those infants who are significantly premature or small-for-gestational age. Children with BPD may require oxygen for months to years. They can also develop heart problems with this disease, and they are much more susceptible to common childhood illnesses and pneumonia. BPD usually improves with age and the growth of new lung tissue.

One of the major changes affecting the heart after birth is the closing of the ductus arteriosus, which connects the pulmonary artery and the aorta while the baby is in the womb. In the preterm infant, this closure may not take place because of the normal tightening of the muscles that lead to closure originates with the increase of oxygen after birth. This is referred to as patent ductus arteriosus. Preterm infants with RDS may not have enough oxygen in the blood to stimulate the closing. This occurs in about 20 percent of those infants born prematurely and weighing less than 2,000 grams. If left uncorrected, the ductus arteriosus can lead to heart failure. The nonsurgical method for correcting this is to tie off the duct. However, medical or surgical alternatives are most often used. The drug Indomethacin is used to stimulate the muscles of the arterial wall to contract. Complications can arise if it decreases urine output or increases bleeding.

Another difficulty for the preterm infant is the immaturity of the central nervous system. The brain stem is the area of the central nervous system which controls the infant's respiratory efforts. Often, the preterm infant will forget to breathe. This is called apnea. The more premature the infant, the more serious the apnea. Newborns who have sustained brain damage due to other complications also are likely to have apnea. Apnea is often treated with the drug, theophylline, which is related to caffeine. When a newborn continues to have episodes of apnea, even after treatment, it may be a sign of brain damage, or a precursor to SIDS, sudden infant death syndrome. SIDS occurs more often in preterm infants than in full-term babies. At this time, there is no preventive treatment for SIDS. Babies who continue to have apnea complications are usually sent home with an apnea monitor which sounds an alarm when the infant stops breathing. Poor nutritional intake can compromise an already immature central nervous system. The preterm infant may not suck or swallow adequately, which may indicate a need for intravenous feedings, or in more long-term situations, feedings by stomach tube.

BIOCHEMICAL ABNORMALITIES

Premature infants tend to have smaller reserves of glucose than the full-term baby, and may be at an increased risk for hypoglycemia. This could lead to vomiting, seizures, and lethargy. These symptoms can be avoided by monitoring blood glucose levels and by giving intravenous glucose.

And, because the premature infant does not have the fatty tissue needed to regulate body temperature adequately, he or she could become hypothermic. This is why incubators are used for the preterm infant.

A biochemical complication is that of intraventricular hemorrhage (IVH), or bleeding into brain tissue and fluid spaces within the brain. IVH is graded from Grade I to Grade IV. Slight leaking of blood is considered Grade I, whereas severe bleeding into the ventricles and surrounding brain tissue is considered Grade IV. Severe bleeding can also lead to blockage, which can result in hydrocephalus, also known as water on the brain. This may require a surgical procedure whereby a tube is placed in the ventricles of the brain to drain the excess fluid. The tube is called a ventricular-peritoneal shunt and runs from the brain to the abdomen, where the fluid is drained.

Retrolental fibroplasia is another possible feature of prematurity. It is caused by an overgrowth of blood vessels in the tissue of the back of the eye or retina. Retrolental fibroplasia is not as common a problem today as it was in the 1940s and 1950s because lower oxygen levels are now used for those preterm infants who have RDS. These babies are also routinely checked by an ophthalmologist while in the special care nursery.

Necrotizing enterocolitis is a condition in which, due to lack of oxygen, part of the infant's bowel ceases to work and is rendered useless. In the more severe cases, the baby is at risk for developing a hole in the bowel, called a perforation, which requires surgical intervention. In milder cases, the problem may resolve itself by withholding regular feedings and having nutrients given directly into the blood vessel. This is referred to as hyperalimentation.

Generally speaking, the earlier a baby is born, and the smaller and less developed he or she is, the greater the risk of complications. Preterm infants as small as one to two pounds, and born as early as the 26th week of gestation, have a chance of surviving today. Just a little over a decade ago, these infants would have had little chance of surviving. However, severely premature infants are still at considerable risk for long-term developmental difficulties.

OTHER NEWBORN COMPLICATIONS

Anencephaly is a condition describing an infant born with major parts of the brain absent. These babies may have enough brain stem activity at birth to breathe and suck for a period. Most will show no developmental progress and die of infection or respiratory distress shortly after birth.

In hydranencephaly, the baby is born with an average size or slightly enlarged skull. However, the spaces inside the skull are filled with fluid instead of brain tissue. Again, the brain stem may function and the infant will breathe and suck for a time, but most of these babies will die within the first few months of the newborn period.

Holoprosencephaly refers to a condition in which the cells that function to form the infant's face and front of the brain do not develop properly. This results in significant brain abnormalities as well as atypical facial features. The eyes are usually set very close together and the nose, if existent, is very small. Also present is a large cleft palate. Those children who survive the newborn period often have uncontrollable seizures and little capacity for intellectual achievement.

Meconium aspiration refers to a condition in which a newborn inhales meconium while taking his first breaths. Meconium is the sticky black material that collects in the fetal intestinal tract before birth and is usually passed during the first few days after birth. Meconium passed before birth into the amniotic fluid, also known as meconium staining, is an indication of fetal distress. Aspiration of the meconium can result in blocked airways leading to respiratory distress.

MORE ABOUT GRADY

At this time, Grady is three and a half years old. He has made progress beyond expectations for a child born with his challenges. He is healthy and attached; most adoptive parents will tell you these are two of the most important components of a successful special needs placement. Grady is still delayed in the areas of expressive language and gross motor skills. He also still has some health problems related to his reactive airway disease. Most of the preschool years with a medically fragile child are spent getting him or her physically healthy. We know we face other challenges with Grady related to the drug and alcohol exposure. However, we have been fortunate in receiving exemplary early intervention services through our local school district.

Most school districts throughout this country have such programs to help differently-abled children get a good start before kindergarten. In fact, federal statues enacted under the Individuals With Disabilities Education Act (IDEA) (P.L.94–142) maintain that all states will provide the necessary educational services for children ages 3-18 who have disabilities. In addition, schools will provide individually designed programs for special needs children at no cost to the parents—that is, free appropriate public education for all children identified as requiring a special education.

Chapter 3

PHYSICAL, NEUROLOGICAL AND GENETIC IMPAIRMENT

The following stories have a common thread, though the children have different challenges. Many differently-abled children have a primary diagnosis which often directly affects other areas of development such as cognitive and motor skills and in communication and processing.

Mike was born with cerebral palsy and severe hearing loss. Because of his communication challenges, it is difficult to assess his true abilities academically and socially. At this time he is doing well in a community school where he works at an age level two years younger than a fully-abled child of nine.

Connie was born with spina bifida. As a result of other medical complications related to the spina bifida, she was not able to begin her physical and occupational therapy in earnest until the age of four, at which time her motor and communications skills increased dramatically.

Katie was born healthy and appeared developmentally on task until shortly before her second birthday. At this time, she simply ceased to speak or make eye contact. She no longer walked or crawled and she cried inconsolably much of the day and night. Katie was eventually diagnosed with the little understood genetic disorder of Rhett syndrome.

Brian was born significantly preterm, which resulted in neurological damage; Brian's challenges are in the areas of cognitive development, visual impairment, and seizure disorder. In spite of his challenges, or perhaps because of them, Brian is an extremely happy and well-adjusted child. He attends a developmental preschool with other differently-abled children. One of the unique features at this school is the emphasis on helping children with multiple disabilities function more independently rather than on traditional academics and developmental sequence, which too often have proven to be ineffective models in the area of special education. Some concepts such as colors or numbers may have no meaning for a child with multiple special needs. A few of the newer models of special education are focusing on helping the children with life skills, such as self-management in buying their own school lunch, reading restroom and exit signs, and developing social skills. For more information on special education models and developmental school settings, refer to Appendix C.

SPINA BIFIDA AND HYOROCEPHALUS

Meningomyelocele, more commonly known as spina bifida, is a defect of the spinal cord and the spinal column. This occurs during the first few weeks of pregnancy when the spinal canal is being formed. The canal does not close as it should, and the spinal cord, all surrounding tissue, and the membranes covering the spinal cord begin to protrude out through the back of the spine. This will, in turn, cause serious damage to the vulnerable nerves in the spinal cord. The end result is paralysis in the lower back. The severity of the paralysis depends upon where the nerves project through the spine. The higher the opening on the infants back, the greater the paralysis. When the opening is around the middle of the back, the child will probably have to use a wheelchair. Some may be able to stand on their own and some may be able to walk short distances. When the lower back is affected, the child will probably be able to walk with braces and crutches. If the damage is at the lowest point of the back, the child will probably do well with lightweight ankle braces, and some may need no assistance at all.

The nerve damage will cause many children to have numbness in the feet, legs, and lower back. It can also affect the child's bladder and bowel control. Urinary tract infections are common with meningomyelocele. Over 90 percent of the children who have spina bifida also have problems with hydrocephalus, which refers to increased fluid in the ventricles of the brain. As the ventricles fill, the head will enlarge and the brain tissue will compress, ultimately causing brain damage.

Infants with spina bifida require immediate surgery. The opening in the back is closed, and a shunt operation is performed if hydrocephalus occurs. If there are no medical complications with these two procedures intellectual development should be normal. However, if there is a shunt malformation or if the infant develops ventriculitis, an infection of the fluid spaces in the brain, his or her cognitive abilities can be affected.

Hydrocephalus can also result from brain injury, infection, bleeding, or tumor. The expected outcome for these children will depend upon the cause, the severity of the condition, and how quickly the condition is treated. Hydrocephalus is treated by surgically implanting a shunt (plastic tube) to channel excess fluid to other parts of the body, where it is absorbed.

CONGENITAL HEART DISEASE

Congenital heart defects fall into two categories: those that cause cyanosis (blue discoloration of the skin, lips and tongue), which is an indication a low level of oxygen in the blood, and noncyanotic heart disease. Cyanotic heart disease is usually detected within a few days after birth.

Tetralogy of Fallot is characterized by an obstruction of blood flow to the lungs and by the mixing of oxygenated and unoxygenated blood. There are four defects in tetralogy of fallot: a narrowed passage between the right ventricle and the pulmonary artery; a thickening of the walls of the right ventricle, caused by the blood flow obstruction; a defect of the wall between the two lower chambers; and a misplacement of the root of the aorta.

Transposition of the great vessels occurs when the arteries that leave the aorta and those from the pulmonary artery are reversed. The right ventricle is connected to the aorta instead of to the pulmonary artery, and the left ventricle is attached to the pulmonary artery instead of the aorta. When this happens, oxygen poor blood is not returned to the lungs to get oxygen. Instead, it is pumped directly into the infant's circulatory system, resulting in cyanosis.

CLEFT PALATE AND CLEFT LIP

Cleft lip and palate occur when there is no joining of the pharyngeal arches during fetal development. This happens in about 1 out of 1000 births, when the cells that should grow together to form lips and palate do not move in the proper direction. This creates an opening, or cleft. When the development occurs in the early stages, the result may be a cleft in the lip only. Cleft lip and palate can occur as an isolated birth defect, or in conjunction with a more complex medical condition. Specific environmental events such as use of drugs, German measles, and vitamin deficiencies have been associated with cleft. Cleft palate can result in the abnormal spacing of teeth, and missing or extra teeth; long-term dental complications, even with surgical closure between 3 months of age. In addition, the formation of various sounds in speech may be labored. Before surgical repair, the cleft interferes with the infant's ability to suck, resulting in immediate feeding problems. Specialized feeders are available for these babies.

A series of surgical procedures are performed, generally within the first year and a half, to correct the palate and lip defect. The child may or may not have speech problems. However, children with cleft lip and palate have a higher tendency toward middle ear infections and conductive hearing loss. Careful follow-up of the child's hearing is necessary. It is essential that particular attention be given these areas in order to prevent future problems with speech, language, and cognitive development.

SEIZURE DISORDERS

Seizures can occur because of trauma, malformations within the brain, inflammation of the brain, tumor, scars, or chemical imbalance. Epilepsy can become the symptom which alerts parents and physicians to these brain abnormalities. Epilepsy is a condition wherein electrical discharges in the brain disrupt the normal functioning of the nervous system. These seizures can result in temporary changes of behavior or in a loss of consciousness, depending on the area of the brain affected.

Generalized seizures affect the whole brain and nearly always bring on a loss of consciousness.

CLEFT PALATE AND CLEFT LIP

Cleft lip and palate occur when there is no joining of the pharyngeal arches during fetal development. This happens in about 1 out of 1000 births, when the cells that should grow together to form lips and palate do not move in the proper direction. This creates an opening, or cleft. When the development occurs in the early stages, the result may be a cleft in the lip only. Cleft lip and palate can occur as an isolated birth defect, or in conjunction with a more complex medical condition. Specific environmental events such as use of drugs, German measles, and vitamin deficiencies have been associated with cleft. Cleft palate can result in the abnormal spacing of teeth; and missing or extra teeth; long-term dental complications, even with surgical closure between 1-2 months of age. In addition, the formation of various sounds in speech may be labored. Before surgical repair, the cleft interferes with the infant's ability to suck, resulting in immediate feeding problems. Specialized feeders are available for these babies.

A series of surgical procedures are performed, generally within the first year and a half, to correct the palate and lip defect. The child may or may not have speech problems. However, children with cleft lip and palate have a higher tendency toward middle ear infections and conductive hearing loss. Careful follow-up of the child's hearing is necessary. It is essential that particular attention be given these areas in order to prevent future problems with speech, language, and cognitive development.

SEIZURE DISORDERS

Seizures can occur because of trauma, malformations within the brain, inflammation of the brain, tumor, scars, or chemical imbalance. Epilepsy can become the symptom which alerts parents and physicians to these brain abnormalities. Epilepsy is a condition wherein electrical discharges in the brain disrupt the normal functioning of the nervous system. These seizures can result in temporary changes of behavior or in a loss of consciousness, depending on the area of the brain affected.

Generalized seizures affect the whole brain and nearly always bring on a loss of consciousness. The four major categories of generalized seizures are: absence seizures, myoclonic seizures, atonic seizures, and tonic/clonic seizures.

Absence seizures are characterized by the brain's normal activity shutting down. A child experiencing an absence seizure may stare blankly, dropping objects, sometimes repetitively jerking or blinking. His or her eyes may rotate upwards and there may be occasional involuntary movements also know as "automatismís. The absence seizure is usually over as fast as it began, generally lasting only a few seconds. However, if a child experiences these type of seizures numerous times a day, it can interfere with school performance. Because these seizures are of such short duration, they can often be misinterpreted as a child not paying attention or simply daydreaming.

Myoclonic seizures are characterized by a sudden jerk which, by itself, can seem relatively mild. However, myoclonic seizures are frequently associated with more severe and increasingly worsening neurological problems. The myoclonic seizure can be confined to individual muscle groups or it can be a tremendous twitch which can throw a child to the ground.

Atonic seizures are characterized by a total slumping of the body due to a complete loss of muscle tone. These are also called "drop attacks." This type of seizure is relatively rare but is often associated with more progressive and serious forms of epilepsy. These children frequently require protective headgear in order to prevent further head or facial injury.

Tonic/clonic seizures are also referred to as "grand mal" convulsions. During such a seizure, a child may cry out and then fall to the ground. The body is extremely rigid during the tonic phase, then will begin to convulse during the clonic stage. This can last anywhere from several seconds to several minutes and is frequently followed by deep sleep or an extended period of confusion. The tonic/clonic seizure can cause a child to bite his tongue and lose bladder control. Often, these seizures will produce muscle soreness and headaches.

Partial seizures are also known as focal or local seizures. They affect limited areas of the brain as opposed to generalized seizures, which begin in the central brain and spread throughout.

Partial seizures fall into two categories: simple partial seizures and complex partial seizures. Simple partial seizures are a result of an abnormal discharge affecting nerve cells responsible for movement. During this type of seizure, the person remains conscious while a localized body part is affected. For example, a leg may begin to jerk, followed by involuntary movement of parts on the same side of the body. If there is a seizure in the sensory part of the brain, there might be abnormal visual phenomena or memory disturbance. This is often followed by feelings of fear, anger, or excitement. Complex partial seizures are much like simple partial seizures with the exception that the discharge affects the part of the brain that controls consciousness. During this type of seizure, the person may experience automatism's, such as lip smacking, chewing or fumbling with objects, which cannot be recalled when the person regains consciousness. In either, simple partial seizures or complex partial seizures, the initial seizure can spread and involve other parts of the brain. At this time, consciousness will be lost and the person may then experience a tonic/clonic seizure. When a seizure begins in one specific location and spreads to affect the whole brain, it is called secondarily generalized seizure.

When seizures occur one right after another, without the person regaining consciousness, the designation used is status epilepticus. This can be a potentially life-threatening event if the seizures are generalized clonic/tonic seizures. Absence seizures of this type have far fewer medical complications. Continuous partial epilepsy is the term used when the status epilepticus involves partial seizures or partial motor seizures.

Epileptic syndromes is the medical term referring to specific symptoms which initially lead parents and caregivers to seek the help of a physician. These are often age-related. Within the category of epileptic syndromes are infantile spasms, lennox-gastaut syndrome, rolandic epilepsy, pyknoleptic petit mal, and juvenile myoclonic epilepsy.

Infantile spasms are considered a severe form of epilepsy. Early diagnosis and treatment are essential. These usually begin between three to six months of age, following normal development up to onset. These seizures are characterized by sudden myoclonic jerks, stiffening of the neck, and severe flexing of the neck and body. Often, these seizures are relatively short and occur in clusters. Generally, the neurological and intellectual development are unaffected. Should these seizures begin earlier than three months of age, the outlook is much poorer.

Lennox-gastaut syndrome is an all-encompassing term that refers to a variety of seizures. These include atonic drop attacks, absence seizures, complex partial seizures, and tonic/clonic seizures. This particular syndrome is often associated with extreme delays in motor and intellectual development. It is difficult to treat and does not respond well to drugs. If these type of seizures are fairly limited, then it is possible to control them medically. However, Lennox-gastaut syndrome is often associated with more serious brain disturbances. If this is the case, then controlling the seizures is much more difficult, which in turn has serious consequences on intellectual development. The overall outlook is determined by the extent and nature of the exact brain disturbance.

Rolandic epilepsy is generally much easier to control with a significantly better prognosis. This type of epilepsy is a partial seizure which occurs within the first ten years of life. It is characterized by partial motor seizures which usually occur when the child is sleeping. It is known to respond positively to drug therapy and generally subsides during adolescence. There is usually no underlying neurological disturbance associated with rolandic epilepsy.

Pyknoleptic petit mal refers to a syndrome of childhood absence seizures with an overall positive outlook. These seizures are characterized by absence attacks, which can actually occur over a hundred times a day. However, it does respond well to medication and often goes away at puberty. These seizures can result from overexertion, sleepiness, or nervousness.

Juvenile myoclonic epilepsy is characterized by generalized tonic/clonic seizures. Often, these occur upon awakening in the morning. These are frequently accompanied by absence seizures and myoclonic jerks. This type of epilepsy responds positively to drug therapy as well.

Febrile seizures are associated with elevated fevers and generally affect 3 to 5 percent of the population. Of this percentage, about half will experience recurrent febrile seizures. Some of these will go on to develop epilepsy in some form. Simple febrile seizures will not require any medication, but if they reoccur consistently, then preventive drug therapy with Phenobarbital or diazepam may be an option.

CEREBRAL PALSY

Cerebral palsy is a general term which covers a variety of disorders that affect a child's ability to move and maintain balance and posture.

These types of disorders are caused by injury to the brain, either before birth, during birth, or within a few years after birth. Because cerebral palsy affects the way a child develops, it is considered a developmental disability. However, depending on the location and severity of the brain injury which can cause these movement disorders, the child may have other problems as well. These include seizures, mental retardation, language disorders, learning disabilities, and visual or hearing impairment. The injury which results in cerebral palsy does not damage the child's muscles or the nerves connecting them to the spinal cord. Rather, it affects the brain's ability to control these muscles.

In the United States, about two children in one thousand are born with some type of cerebral palsy. More children are born with cerebral palsy than with any other developmental disability, including Down syndrome, epilepsy, or autism.

Cerebral palsy is usually a lifelong disability, though problems and physical movement associated with cerebral palsy may change with age, growth, and therapeutic intervention. This also depends upon the type of cerebral palsy with which a child is affected. When describing specific types of movement disorders associated with cerebral palsy, medical professionals use a variety of terms and classification labels. All children with cerebral palsy have a certain amount of damage to the area of the brain that controls muscle tone. This results in either increased muscle tone, decreased muscle tone, or fluctuating muscle tone. So, some of the most common terms used in describing types of cerebral palsy have to do with muscle tone, or the amount of tension in a given muscle.

High tone (spasticity) is the term used to describe children who have an increased muscle tone. This is characterized by stiff and awkward movements due to the increased tension within the muscles. Infants with high tone muscles tend to arch their backs and have stiff extended legs. Because of this stiffness, they may roll over in one solid flip as opposed to more fluid rolling motions. They also may begin doing this at an earlier age, such as one month instead of the normal three to five months. When they begin standing, they tend to scissor their legs and stand stiffly on their toes.

Children with decreased tone are said to have low tone, or hypotonia. This is characterized by an inability of the child to maintain positions because the muscles are floppy because they do not contract or they are too relaxed. These infants lie on their backs with their arms, legs, and head resting on the floor or bed. They are often unable to remain upright. When in a sitting position, they tend to lean forward with a rounded back. Low tone will also affect the child's ability to reach or hold on to objects. When the hypotonia affects the abdominal muscles, it can causes delays and impairment in the development of speech and language.

There are some children who have a combination of high tone and low tone. This is referred to as fluctuating or variable muscle tone. Children with fluctuating tone may have low tone when they are sleeping or at rest, and experience high tone when active and moving about.

There are three classifications of cerebral palsy based upon the location of the brain injury: pyramidal (spastic) cerebral palsy, extrapyramidal (choreoatheoid) cerebral palsy, and mixed-type cerebral palsy.

Pyramidal cerebral palsy is diagnosed most often. It affects about 50 percent of the children with cerebral palsy. These children have one or more tight muscle groups which restrict movement. A child with spastic or pyramidal cerebral palsy has received damage to the part of the brain which controls voluntary movement. There may be damage to the pathways that connect the motor cortex with the nerves in the spinal cord which in turn relays motor signals to the muscles. When the pyramidal tracts or motor cortex are damaged, the brain has difficulty receiving or sending messages to either or both sides of the body.

Spastic cerebral palsy is also characterized by one or more of the following: ankle clonus—the muscles in the calf and foot suddenly and rhythmically contract when the calf muscles are flexed and the foot is pointing upward, or when the child is in a standing position; contractures - this is the abnormal shortening of tendons and muscles around certain joints due to lack of full movement and tight muscles; exaggerated stretch reflexes—when reflexes are tested with a reflex hammer, they respond faster and more pronounced than normal; persistent primitive reflexes—these are involuntary movements brought on by touch, pressure or stimulation which can last up to months and even years; Positive Babinski—this is when the toes on a child one year or older extend and fan out rather than flex when the foot is stroked from heel to toes.

About one-fourth of the children with cerebral palsy have extrapyramidal (choreoathetoid) cerebral palsy. This occurs when there is damage to the cerebellum or basal ganglia. When these areas are damaged, the child may have involuntary movements in the face, arms, and trunk. This often results in difficulty feeding, speaking, reaching, or grasping. When there is involuntary movement in the face, there may be drooling, slurred speech, and difficulty swallowing.

Extrapyramidal cerebral palsy is characterized by one or more of the following: athetosis—slow, writhing movements most noticeable in the hands and face; ataxia—a lack of coordination when standing or walking caused by damage to the cerebellum; chorea—jerky-type movements in the head, neck, arms, or legs; dystonia—slow, twisting-type movements in the trunk, arms, or legs; and rigidity—high muscle tone and restricted movements.

It is not unusual for an infant to be nine months of age or older before parents and physicians notice and diagnose this type of cerebral palsy.

Mixed-type cerebral palsy occurs in about one-fourth of the children with cerebral palsy. It is characterized by the spastic muscle tone of pyramidal cerebral palsy and the involuntary movements of extrapyramidal cerebral palsy. These children have damage to the areas of the brain which affect both pyramidal and extrapyramidal function.

When determining the specific type of cerebral palsy with which a child is affected, physicians look at how the cerebral palsy influences the nervous system. Depending on the problem areas of movement, the cerebral palsy will be classified as one of the following: monoplegia, diplegia, hemiplegia, quadraplegia, or double hemiplegia.

Monoplegia is the term used when the cerebral palsy affects only one arm or leg on one side of the body. This is an extremely mild form of cerebral palsy and can disappear with time.

Diplegia refers to cerebral palsy that is concentrated in a child's legs. These children have a tendency to stand on their toes and scissor their legs. They may also have mild muscle tone problems in the upper part of their body.

Hemiplegia means that one side of the child's body is affected by cerebral palsy. The arm and leg on the affected side may be shorter and less developed. Use of the hand on this side depends upon the degree of impairment and amount of sensation. About 50 percent of the children with hemiplegia experience a loss of sensation on the affected side.

Quadriplegia is the term used when the cerebral palsy affects a child's entire body. Quadriplegia can cause significant difficulty in feeding and speaking because it affects the facial muscles. Though it impresses upon almost all parts of the body, quadriplegia cerebral palsy primarily impairs the child's legs and feet. However, because of its all-encompassing nature, children with quadriplegia experience difficulty in almost all activities associated with basic daily living.

Double Hemiplegia also affects a child's entire body; however, impairment is located more within the child's arms. These children, too, have difficulty with speech and feeding.

The same brain injuries that cause the movement impairments associated with cerebral palsy often contribute to other problem areas and disabilities as well. Brain injury can cause mental retardation, seizure disorders, sensory impairment, and learning disabilities.

MUSCLE AND BONE DISEASES AND BONY DEFORMITIES

Bony deformities can occur in utero or after birth. The two most common bony deformities are congenital dislocation of the hip and club foot. Hip dislocation is seen more often in girls, and is frequently associated with a breech birth, resulting in a mishaped pelvis. This will cause the femur to fit improperly into the socket. Usually adaptive eqipment can be used to correct the problem without any need for surgery.

Club foot is seen more often in boys, and generally is the result of a defect during fetal development. One or both feet turn in, resulting in a poor range of movement. Club foot can be corrected with casting or corrective surgery.

Other bony impairments can involve the entire skeleton. The most common example of this is anchondroplasia, also known as short-limbed dwarfism. A child with this disorder will have shortened arms and legs. This is an inherited disorder and a parent with anchondroplasia will have approximately a 50 percent chance of passing it on to a child.

Other bony complications can occur after birth and are usually associated with another primary disorder. For example, it is not uncommon for a child with cerebral palsy to dislocate a hip because of a strain on various muscles. Children with cerebral palsy and those with frequent bone dislocations are also more likely to suffer from painful arthritis. Arthritis is a condition in which the cartilage around a bony joint is damaged. The joint then loses lubrication and becomes smaller, causing the bones to rub against one another resulting in inflamation, decreased mobility, and frequent pain.

MUSCULAR DYSTROPHIES

One of my favorite stories is that of a parent whose son was diagnosed with muscular dystrophy as a toddler. During his early years, she encouraged him to join in regular activities with other children. At one point, he decided he wanted to play baseball like other neighborhood children. Though her community had no recreation programs for differently-abled children, she took the initiative and formed a T-ball team specifically for children with physical and mental challenges. Eventually, the program grew to include other activities such as swimming, bowling, and family gatherings. This story illustrates how parents can find positive solutions when community or school programs do not have the resources or simply do not realize the need for special needs programs.

Muscular dystrophies are a group of inherited disorders which affect the muscle tissue. These impairments involve a gradual degeneration of the muscles.

Duchenne Muscular Dystrophy is the most common of the group and almost always affects boys. It is noticeable within the first few years after birth. Symptoms include a wide-stanced gait and frequent falling. Because of the progressive deterioration of the muscle, most children will need the use of a wheelchair within about five years after onset. Heart muscles and those used for breathing may weaken as well, which can lead to frequent illness.

Other less serious forms of muscular dystrophy are facioscapulo-humeral muscular dystrophy, limb girdle muscular dystrophy, and becker muscular dystrophy.

Facioscapulohumeral muscular dystrophy primarily involves the muscles in the shoulders and face. It is generally one of the milder forms of the disease. In limb girdle muscular dystrophy, the pelvic muscles are weakened. With this form of the disease, the prognosis varies greatly.

Becker muscular dystrophy is more closely related to Duchenne muscular dystrophy, with much milder symptoms and a better long-term prognosis. Children with this form of the disease are usually able to walk and maintain physical ability into adolescence, and in some cases, early adulthood.

MISSING LIMBS AND PROSTHESES

Renny was born on his due date and healthy in every medical way. However, his parents were initally devastated when they realized he had a withered arm and no hand. They soon turned this energy into action and within four months after his birth, Renny was fitted with his first prosthesis. Their initial concerns that he would not be able to engage in the activities of his peer group were dispelled one by one as he learned to ride a bike, tie his shoes, and join in organized sports.

Prosthetics, nonmoving models and those which are electrically controlled, are expensive due to the small numbers needed. According to the federal Centers for Disease Control and Prevention, 1,500 to 2,000 children are born each year with a limb deficiency.

Children can be born with malformation of the limbs which can include missing parts, shortened limbs and malformed or atypical limbs. Malignant tumors and trauma may necessitate the amputation of a limb. In these cases, prosthetic devices or artificial body parts may be needed.

Prosthetics for lower limbs such as the foot, ankle, lower leg, or entire leg aid in restoring proper balance. Prostheses for arms or hands help a child with routine activities such as dressing, feeding, handling objects, and interaction in play and sports. Prosthetic equipment can also be important to a child's self-image and appearance. All prosthetics are individualized and are fitted and made by a trained prosthetist, in accordance with a doctor's prescription. Artificial body parts are made to resemble the missing limb and to match the corresponding limb.

DOWN SYNDROME

Rusty was diagnosed with Down syndrome shortly after birth. He was an active child in spite of a heart defect common in people with Down syndrome. As he was growing up he needed several surgeries for the heart defect and to repair some nasal passage difficulties. Rusty attended neighborhood schools, sometimes in special education programs, but more often in mainstream classes. He learned to read at an early age and was active in church youth activies through junior and senior high school. Today he is employed and shares a home with several other developmentally disabled adults. Rusty was fortunate in having a strong family support unit that never underestimated his ability and always encouraged him to be involved in school, community, and church activities.

Down syndrome is a chromosomal disorder. It occurs when an infant is born with 47 chromosomes instead of 46. Of all disorders, only cerebral palsy is more common. Over six thousand babies with Down syndrome are born in the United States each year. It occurs in boys and girls evenly. Babies with Down syndrome possess an extra number-21 chromosome; all of their other chromosomes are normal. The additional chromosomal material causes a genetic imbalance which will alter the course of the development of the fetus.

Newborns with Down syndrome will often have features which will impel initial testing. If Down syndrome is suspected, karyotypes (a picture of human chromosomes which can reveal the presence of extra genetic material) and other tests are ordered.

Down syndrome infants may have some of the following facial features: the nasal bridge of the nose tends to be flatter. The nose and the nasal passages may be smaller, which can cause congestion more easily; the eyes often slant upward and have small folds of skin called, "epicanthal folds" around the inner corners. The outer part of the iris may have light spots, referred to as "brushfield spots." These spots do not affect the infant's sight, although vision problems are common among Down syndrome children; the mouth may be small and the roof of the mouth may be shallow. This can cause the tongue to protrude and appear large. The teeth usually come in late and in unusual order; they are often small, as well. The ears tend to be small and may fold over. At times, they are set lower on the head. Their size can cause the ear passages to become blocked more easily, leading to hearing loss. Down syndrome children tend to have smaller than normal heads and the back may be flatter. The hands may be smaller with short fingers, and the palm often has one crease across it called a transverse palmer crease. There may be a gap between the first and second toes, although the feet generally appear normal. Down syndrome newborns may have low muscle tone which refers to relaxed and floppy muscles. Often, this is the feature which will initiate the process of looking for other signs of Down syndrome in a newborn.

Babies with Down syndrome do have mental disabilities, though the degree of disability varies greatly among Down syndrome children. However, early intervention and education can enhance the possibilities of achievement for those children with Down syndrome. Often, children with Down syndrome can grow up to live independently or semi-independently. Many Down syndrome adults hold jobs and are contributing members to their communities.

Men with Down syndrome are unable to reproduce; however, women with Down syndrome can reproduce and their eggs often carry the extra number-21 chromosome, leaving them with an increased risk of having a Down syndrome baby.

CYSTIC FIBROSIS

Cystic fibrosis is an autosomal recessive disorder. It is a serious illness which generally shortens a child's life expectancy. The disease causes atypically heavy secretions which lead to chronic lung damage and a lack of enzymes needed to break down and absorb fats. This often leads to malnutrition.

SICKLE CELL ANEMIA

Sickle cell anemia is an autosomal recessive disorder. It is characterized by sickle-shaped, red blood cells. It is a serious disorder which places a child at risk to many bacterial infections due to the spleen not functioning properly. Other symptoms include fever; pain throughout the body due to the lack of blood flow, especially in the joint areas;

and aplastic anemia. Sickle cell is an incurable disease and occurs primarily in African Americans.

FRAGILE X SYNDROME

Fragile X is another genetic disorder which falls under the category of X-linked disorders. Fragile X almost always causes mild to severe mental retardation. Children with fragile X usually have large heads with a prominent forehead, nose, jaw, and ears. Other symptoms include heart murmurs, strabismus, ADHD, and autistic-type behavior. Fragile X is considered the most common genetic cause of mental retardation.

TAY-SACHS DISEASE

Tay-Sachs is considered an autosomal recessive disorder. The origin of Tay-Sachs has been traced to Jewish families living in eastern Poland in the early 1800s. Tay-Sachs did not exist before this period. It is characterized by a failure to thrive, blindness, seizures, and progressive paralysis. These symptoms begin around the age of six months and usually result in death by the age of four. The disorder is caused by a deficiency of the enzyme hexosaminidase, which leads to an accumulation of a material that damages the brain.

HEMOPHILIA

Hemophilia is an X-linked genetic disorder. It is a disease characterized by an inability of the blood to clot. Even minor injury or accident can lead to uncontrolled bleeding. Children with hemophilia usually have numerous chronic disabilities and are frequently hospitalized.

DIABETES

Diabetes Mellitus is a genetically-determined disease. It can appear at any time during childhood for children who have a genetic predisposition to the disease. It is characterized by an insufficient production of insulin restricting a child's ability to metabolize carbohydrates. Children with juvenile onset diabetes usually require daily injections of insulin. Other symptoms include excessive thirst, increased appetite with unexplained weight loss, frequent urination, nausea, vomiting, blurred vision, skin infections, and frequent bladder infections.

As we have seen from the stories of the children mentioned throughout this chapter, many physical and mental challenges overlap into other areas of need. Medical advances in recent years have enabled children with multible disabilities to survive. More children with complicated needs are entering regular and developmental classes across the country. As a result, many special education models are now being reworked. Resources, education, and support in the areas of developmental disabilities have greatly improved over the years.

Chapter 4

VIRAL, BACTERIAL AND INFECTIOUS DISEASES

DJ'S STORY

DJ was born full term and healthy. He was developmentally on target for his first seven months. Just before his eighth month, DJ was hospitalized with a severe case of viral meningitis. DJ suffered significant neurological damage due to the infection. He began having seizures which were several minutes in length. He was diagnosed with mild cerebral palsy and it was determined that he was cortically blind. His seizures continued even after his release from the hospital. Twice, in the next two-year period, he had seizures that lasted up to ten minutes and required medical intervention. Eventually, after much trial and error, medication began to help control the larger seizures, though he still continued to have milder ones occasionally. At age 2 1/2, he was placed in a residential facility for children with visual impairment. He made some improvement in the areas of walking and other gross motor skills. However, he was hospitalized again, this time for a heart defect needing repair and to have tubes put in his ear canals due to frequent infections. After another lengthy recuperation, he began attending a developmental preschool five mornings a week where the emphasis was on learning to get around his home and school, and in areas of social development.

DJ's first five years were spent just trying to get healthy from all of the medical and physical challenges he faced as a result of the meningitis. He is a gregarious and happy child and he made great strides from the time he entered preschool until kindergarten. It was at this age that his progress began to peak somewhat. The elementary years are often the first time that more significant academic and social chal-

36

lenges are recognized. Though he had done well in preschool, he struggled in the kindergarten setting. His foster parents and teachers realized he had picked up many self-management skills and his vocabulary had increased, but he showed no original thought; he merely echoed phrases or words previously said to him. He never initiated conversation or activity with other children. His previously learned skills began more sporadically. Some mornings he dressed himself and on others he would show up at the breakfast table apparently oblivious that he had nothing on. He began to exhibit some autistic-type repetitive behaviors as well.

Today, DJ is almost seven and his caregivers are still unsure of his future potential. His progress is slow, but his heart is big and he readily faces each day. He enjoys school immensely as he faces new challenges in learning Braille and more independence. He recently moved from a neighborhood school to a developmental kindergarten where he receives help from a vision specialist, as well as additional aid in speech and occupational therapy. His foster parents and those who have seen him overcome so many medical challenges consider him a true miracle child and though he may not meet the same developmental milestones of his peer group, he has greatly enriched the lives of those around him.

CAUSES OF INFECTION

An infection is an invasion of the body or a specific part of the body by microorganisms, also known as germs, that multiply and cause disease. Infections can be viral, bacterial, or parasitic. They can affect children prenatally or postnatally.

Immunizations help in preventing many serious ill effects children used to suffer due to infection. Measles, whooping cough, diphtheria, tetanus, and poliomyelitis are all infections that have been averted by immunization.

However, there still remain many infections which can cause serious developmental problems in infants and children. The first trimester is a critical period of fetal development. At this time, the basic structure of the body and the brain are being formed. The embryo is particularly susceptible to infections, especially those that can attack the brain and nervous system. If, shortly after birth, an infant is thought to have contracted a prenatal infection, physicians will ask for a TORCH titer. T stands for toxoplasmosis, O for other germs, R for rubella or German measles, C for cytomegalic inclusion disease, and H for herpes simplex. If a high antibody titer for one of the organisms appears, there is a high probability that the infant contracted a prenatal infection. The TORCH is a test which requires blood samples from both mother and infant. The samples are then studied for antibodies against TORCH organisms. If meningitis or encephalitis are suspected, either a spinal tap or lumbar puncture will be conducted. Both tests involve injecting a needle between the spinal cord and its membranes in order to withdraw some spinal fluid which is then examined for bacterial and viral infections.

Long-term prognosis and effects on the child will depend upon the specific infection, the severity of the illness, and the type of treatment received. Antibiotics are usually the first course of action; however, in the cases of cytomegalo-virus or rubella virus, the injury is most often irreversible by birth.

MENINGITIS

Meningitis is an infection of the membranes covering the brain, spinal cord, and adjoining neural tissue. Meningitis can result from many different types of bacteria and the severity of the infection depends on the nature of bacteria, the age of the child, and the effectiveness of the treatment. Children can recover completely from certain meningitis infections, while more severe forms of the illness can cause deafness, blindness, seizures, mental retardation, or paralysis.

ENCEPHALITIS

Encephalitis is considered a viral infection in most cases. The infection causes inflammation of the brain tissue which in turn can lead to seizures, paralysis, mental retardation, or coma. The long-term prognosis depends upon the child's age, the severity of the illness, and the specific type of infection.

Encephalomyelitis is another form of the disease wherein both the brain and spinal cord are infected. Meningoencephalitis is an infection of the brain and its covering membranes. "Sleeping sickness" is the once familiar term used to describe the prolonged coma sometimes caused by the more severe forms of the infection. Brain injury, as a result of encephalitis, can lead to developmental disabilities and behavior disorders.

Childhood illnesses such as mumps and rubella can bring about encephalitis as can the herpes simplex virus.

HERPES SIMPLEX

Herpes Simplex are virus infections. Type 1 is referred to a oral herpes. Type 2 is known as genital herpes, which is spread by sexual contact. Newborns can contract type 2 when passing through an infected birth canal. A cesarean delivery can prevent infection. An infant infected with type 2 herpes simplex will usually show symptoms within the first couple of months after birth. Symptoms may include milder forms of skin rashes to more serious infection of major organs including the brain. This can lead to mental retardation and sometimes death.

TOXOPLASIA

Toxoplasia is a parasitic infection, with cats being the primary host. These parasites can be found throughout the world, and the infection is spread through contaminated feces or with improperly cooked meat. When the infection is passed on to an unborn baby, the result is generally premature birth and an infant who is small-for-gestational age. Infected infants and children face the possibility of visual impairment, mental retardation, and sometimes, early infant death. An infected child may have an unusually small or large head.

CYTOMEGALIC INCLUSION DISEASE

Cytomegalic Inclusion Disease, often referred to as CMV, is a common virus also found throughout the world. Though most infants who are infected in utero show no symptoms at birth, they are at a greater risk for hearing impairment at a later age. Newborns who do show symptoms at birth usually display the following: small-for-gestational age, blood spots on the skin, jaundice, developmental delay, and a possibility of mental retardation.

RUBELLA

Rubella, more commonly known as German measles, is rarely seen anymore due to immunizations. Most states require women to undergo a premarital blood test before issuing a marriage license. This test is to determine her immunity to rubella. Rubella is usually contracted from other infected humans through coughing or moist breath. Infants, infected prenatally, may be small-for-gestational age, have a hearing or visual impairment, be at risk for congenital heart disease, microcephalic, or mentally retarded.

HEPATITIS

Hepatitis is a viral infection of the liver. The two most commonly seen hepatitis viruses are Hepatitis A and Hepatitis B. Any form of the hepatitis virus will include symptoms of fatigue, loss of appetite, dark urine, and, in many cases, fever. An enlarged liver will cause the white of the eyes and skin to take on a yellow cast. A person can have hepatitis one time and never have any problems with it again, or they can suffer bouts of chronic infection.

Hepatitis A is often referred to as infectious hepatitis and is a one-time infection. It is transmitted through fecal contaminated drink or food. Once a person has had hepatitis A he or she is immune to further infections and is not a carrier. All that is required for the person infected with type A is bed rest.

Hepatitis B is also known as HBV. Type B can occur in two separate stages. Immediately after becoming infected, a person can go through an acute stage which can last anywhere from several weeks to several months. The symptoms include lack of appetite, nausea and vomiting, fatigue, stomach pain, dark urine, rashes, and yellow-tinted skin. However, over half of the people who are infected with type B never experience the acute stage. Many never realize they are carriers and can spread the infection to others. A person can contract HBV through bodily secretions. These include sex, razors, toothbrushes, or sharing needles used to inject drugs. At this time, there is no treatment for acute hepatitis; the person with chronic HBV can be treated with Intron A which cures about 40 percent of those infected.

Immunizations can protect approximately 95 percent of the people who receive the entire series of three injections. This set of vaccines will lasts about ten years. It is very important for infants to be vaccinated against HBV during their first year. The younger a child is at the time they are infected, the more likely he or she is to become a carrier.

TUBERCULOSIS

Tuberculosis, also referred to as TB, is a bacterial infection. About 30 years ago, TB was almost eradicated in the U.S. due to antituberculous drugs. However, there has been a recent resurgence which is probably AIDS related. TB is spread through a cough. The bacteria from TB infects the lungs and the moisture from a cough can carry the infection to another who inhales the droplets. Unpasteurized milk is another possible source of TB infection. Most of those infected with TB show no symptoms. Those who are symptomatic may experience a persistent cough with blood, fatigue, fever, sweats, and loss of appetite and weight. A tuberculosis infection requires aggressive drug therapy and can be cured, though it is usually fatal if left untreated. A urine test or the Mantoux intradermal skin test can detect TB.

For those considering international adoption both TB and Hepatitis B should be thoroughly studied and considered. They tend to be more prevalent in crowded living conditions such as orphanages.

HIV AND AIDS

Human immunodeficiency virus (HIV) is the virus that results in acquired immunodeficiency syndrome (AIDS). The HIV infection can be contracted through intimate sexual contact with an infected partner and intravenous drug use with contaminated needles. Prior to screening tests, HIV could be passed through transfusion with infected blood or blood products. Pregnant women who are HIV positive have a 30 - 50 percent chance of having a baby who is also infected with the virus. HIV can pass through breast milk as well; infected mothers should not breast feed.

When an HIV infection develops into AIDS, the virus attacks cells that are necessary in fighting other infections. A diagnosis of AIDS is based on a blood test confirming HIV infection, significantly decreased levels of immunity, and recurrent and severe infections. Children with AIDS often contract lymphoid interstitial pneumonia and pneumocystis carinii pneumonia.

An HIV antibody test and other diagnostic testing is usually required to determine the HIV status of a newborn. Most infected infants will develop symptoms by the age of two. Developmental delays and disabilities may result from progressive neurological impairment, repeated infections, and multiple hospitalizations.

Chapter 5

SENSORY DISORDERS

VISUAL IMPAIRMENT

Andrew is another young man who faces the challenges of visual impairment. Like DJ, Andrew is cortically blind due to neurological dysfunction. Andrew is considered legally blind, although he has a moon shape sliver of sight in the bottom of both eyes. For this reason he tends to walk with his head up so as to use this vision as much as he can. When Andrew first was placed in a new foster home, his foster parents immediately enlisted the aid of the local elementary school media specialist for reading resources. As is often the situation with people who are not familiar with visual impairment, the idea was that the bigger the print of a book, the better. Andrew's foster parents soon learned this is not necessarily the case, especially in cases of cortical blindness. Actually, in Andrew's case, the smaller the print and pictures, the more recognizable they were to him. When he looked at large print he was only able to see a portion of the letter which meant nothing to him in term of recognition. Another challenge Andrew's foster parents faced was that of differing philosophies in how to approach education with a visually impaired child. Andrew's previous foster parents had wanted him to appear as typical as other nonvisually impaired children. For this reason, they decided against Andrew learning Braille and put their efforts into teaching him to read with the small portion of vision he had.

His new foster parents felt that Andrew was having to put so much effort into trying to see and recognize letters that his eyes strained easily which made learning to read a tedious and unenjoyable activity. They chose the route of having a vision specialist teach Andrew and the entire family Braille. Soon the parents had Braille labels taped on

43

objects throughout the home. Underneath the Braille type on each label, they wrote the word in marker. In this way Andrew began piecing written words and related Braille together. Reading and learning seemed to become a more exciting experience for Andrew.

Ryan had no visual impairment until he was traumatically shaken by a caregiver at the age of six. His vision was limited all through school until his junior year when he lost his sight altogether on the football field. Being an athletic person, Ryan had a very difficult time adjusting to the complete loss. Soon, however, a dedicated caseworker introduced him to tandem bike riding. With a sighted partner, Ryan was able to keep physically active and enjoy weekend bike marathons. Today, Ryan has a seeing eye dog to help in his continued effort toward independence.

There are many causes and degrees of visual impairment. Impairment can result from congenital abnormalities, metabolic disease, genetic disorders, injuries, accidents, or illnesses. Nearsightedness (myopia) and farsightedness (hyperopia) are two of the more common and milder conditions of visual impairment. Both are usually corrected with contact lenses or glasses.

Other, more serious visual impairments include the following:

1. Retinitis pigmentosa, which is a result of atypical accumulation pigment.

2. Retinoblastoma is a tumor of the eye.

3. Cataracts. Though more often associated with the elderly, infants can be born with cataracts and young children can develop them as well. Cataracts enlarge over time and cause the eye lens to become opaque.

4. Damaged optic nerve which can result in the brain being unable to receive light impulses.

5. Brain damage. Visual impairment can occur when the parts of the brain that interpret visual messages are damaged.

6. Muscle damage. Problems with vision can result from an imbalance in the eye muscles.

7. Strabismus is a condition common in infants. The two types of strabismus include esotropia, which is crossed eyes, and exotropia which is wall-eyes, or eyes that turn out.

8. Amblyopia is more commonly referred to as "lazy eye."

This is a result of one eye becoming more dominant and the brain ignores messages from the other eye to avoid double vision.

9. Nystagmus is a condition wherein there is atypical eye movement, such as a jerky vertical, horizontal or circular motion.

10. Retrolental fibroplasia or retinopathy of prematurity can result from a premature infant requiring extensive and prolonged oxygen. The retina becomes damaged and is unable to appropriately respond to light.

For the child who is totally blind, the onset of blindness plays an important role in other developmental areas. A child blind from birth will generally have more difficulty with motor skills because they are unable to see the movements of others. These children will also have more difficulty with spatial relationships such as large and small. The more severely visually impaired child will need to be able to explore through touch. Touching and other senses are often considered more highly developed as a child compensates for the loss of vision.

HEARING IMPAIRMENT

Whenever my husband and I go through the adoption exchange listings, it is not unusual to notice that an overwhelming majority of the children have special needs in the areas of sensory impairment, especially in the areas of visual and hearing impairment.

In special needs programs many children have been prenatally exposed to substance abuse. In turn, many of these children are preterm or their development in utero is affected, which makes them more susceptible to neurological damage, seizure disorders, cerebral palsy, or a combination of the three. As was noted in previous chapters, these areas of challenge often affect sensory development.

The more common causes of hearing impairment in children often are a result of head injuries and ear infections. Though generally temporary, hearing loss in a child can be caused by chronic middle ear infections. School performance can be greatly affected by this type of impairment, especially if parents and teachers are unaware of a possible hearing loss.

Another temporary cause of hearing problems is the buildup of cerumen (wax) in the ear canal. When the canal is completely blocked, sounds do not reach the eardrum.

More serious hearing loss can result from sensorineural impairment. Impairment can be inherited. In these cases, the child is most often born deaf. Viral infections during the earlier stages of pregnancy can impair an infant's ability to hear, as can the use of certain drugs or medications by the birth mother

A lack of oxygen during birth can cause damage to the brain and result in sensorineural impairment. The use of certain antibiotics such as streptomycin can result in hearing loss. More serious childhood illnesses such as bacterial meningitis are often associated with later hearing loss.

Sensorineural hearing impairment can also be caused by excessive noise which can lead to a permanent hearing loss. Approximately 1 in every 1,000 children has a profound hearing impairment. An estimated 65 percent of these children are born deaf. Another 20 to 30 children in 1,000 have mild to moderate hearing loss. Hearing impairments are often associated with other types of disabilities. Though ear infections can be treated medically, sensorineural hearing impairments are permanent.

Children with hearing loss often have some learning delays as well. The extent of language delays depends upon the severity of hearing loss. Many profoundly hearing impaired children can learn to communicate through sign language, voice synthesizer, or communication boards. Most of these children will require special education and can benefit from early intervention programs.

SENSATION IMPAIRMENT

Nerve injury and paralysis can result in difficulty in feeling various sensations. Changes in temperature, vibrations, touch, and positioning are all sensations that can be affected. Sensation impairment can be temporary or permanent and it can affect specific sensations or be all-encompassing.

The causes of sensation impairment include damage to the brain, which involves the motor system; nerve injury such as spina bifida; injury, disability, or disease that affects the sensory receptors or nerves; and a medical condition referred to as congenital insensitivity to pain.

Illness may cause temporary sensation impairment that will improve with medical treatment. Permanent sensation impairment generally requires ongoing physical therapy.

Chapter 6

COMMUNICATION AND LEARNING DISORDERS

DEFINITION

The presence of a communication or learning disorder, also referred to as a "learning disability," interferes with the learning process. To be able to effectively learn, a child must have the ability to record information being received; process, remember and retrieve the information; and communicate the information. Children should be able to manage these tasks through all conduits of communication. These are visual, auditory, and tactile. When one of the processes is impaired, learning becomes much more difficult and complicated. When a child has a learning disability there is usually a discrepancy between ability and his or her intellectual capacity. Often, there are underlying abnormalities in the cognitive process which either precede or are found in conjunction with learning and communication disorders. These include visual perception, memory, attention, and language deficits. Learning disorders are common in a wide variety of medical conditions such as fetal alcohol effects or syndrome, lead poisoning, neurological impairment, and fragile X syndrome. However, there are many children who have learning or communication disorders with no such medical history.

EXPRESSIVE LANGUAGE DISORDER

Expressive language disorder is characterized by a child's inability to comprehend and express vocal or sign language.

There are also deficits in sensory perception (recognizing sounds) or in visual symbols (pictures), as well as an inability to recognize and

47

organize related auditory or visual symbols. Sequencing (reproducing in consecutive order) and short-term memory are affected by this disorder. Other features include shortened sentences, limited amount of speech, small range of vocabulary, limited grammatical structures and difficulty in learning new words. Expressive language disorder seriously affects the child's academic achievement. Some children with expressive language problems may have slight delays in the development of motor skills. Reading and spelling difficulties are also prevalent.

RECEPTIVE-EXPRESSIVE LANGUAGE DISORDER

In receptive-expressive language disorder, there is impairment in both receptive and expressive language development. The difficulties may occur in verbal communication or sign language. This disorder seriously affects academic achievement.

The child with receptive-expressive language difficulties will have a limited vocabulary, trouble recalling words or using sentences with developmentally appropriate length, difficulty in expressing ideas, and inability to understand many age appropriate words and sentences. Auditory processing deficits often accompany this disorder.

PHONOLOGICAL DISORDER

This communication disorder is characterized by a child's inability to develop consistent articulations of the more sophisticated speech sounds, such as ch, f, l, r, sh, th, or z. These children often sound as if they are using "baby talk" when they verbalize. Vocabulary and grammatical structuring are usually age appropriate; however, slight reading delays may be present.

STUTTERING

The distinguishing feature of stuttering is a disturbance in the normal or expected fluency and time patterning of speech considered

developmentally appropriate. There are frequent repetitions and pro-
longations of words, syllables, or sounds.

This disorder interferes with social interaction and academic
achievement. Other features of stuttering may include word substitu-
tion in order to avoid problem words, pauses in speech, broken words,
pauses within words, interjections, excess tension used to produce certain words, and entire word repetition. The severity of the problem
varies with each individual and stress can exacerbate the disturbance.
Often, stuttering is absent during singing, oral reading, and talking to
inanimate objects or to pets.

READING DISORDER

The presenting feature of this disorder is a significant impairment in
a child's development of reading skills, taking into consideration
chronological age, mental age, and formal education. Reading skills
significantly below the child's intellectual functioning is a secondary
feature.

Often, this disorder is referred to as dyslexia. When reading, a child
may inexplicably omit, add, or distort words. Oral reading is slow and
labored, and reading comprehension is impaired. A child's ability to
copy printed material is usually unaffected. Other characteristics of
this disorder may include language difficulties, numerous errors in
spelling, word sequencing difficulties, and behavioral problems.

EXPRESSIVE WRITING DISORDER

This disorder is characterized by a child's inability to encode
(express) thoughts, emotions, and descriptions in a written form which
is age appropriate. In addition, the child's performance on written
tasks falls significantly below intellectual capacity. Other associated
features of this impairment may include reading and spelling difficulties, the inability to sequence consecutively, and deficits in short-term
memory.

MATHEMATICS DISORDER

The identifying characteristic of this disorder is a child's inability to develop expected arithmetic skills with same-aged peers. The child performs significantly below intellectual capacity on tasks involving arithmetic skills. This disorder is often associated with other learning disabilities in the areas of reading and spelling. Mathematics disorder is not as prevalent as the other learning and communication disorders

Communication and learning disorders are most often treated within the educational system. Generally, children who have a learning or communication disorder have no other association with a psychopathological disorder.

In most cases involving a learning or communication disorder, the related difficulties continue throughout childhood and adolescence and into adulthood. Academic performance is invariably affected when there is a learning and communication disorder. Impairment is more notably marked when there is dysfunction in the areas of language and articulation.

DEVELOPMENTAL COORDINATION DISORDER

Children with developmental motor coordination disorder may have difficulties in fine motor or gross motor skills. Fine motor involves skills which require the coordination of the small muscles of the body, including those of the hands and face. Fine motor skills include such tasks as drawing, handwriting, stacking small blocks, stringing beads, tracking an object with the eyes, etc.

Gross motor involves the developmental area of skills which require the coordination of large muscle groups, such as the arms, legs, and trunk. These tasks include walking, jumping, and throwing a ball. Fine motor disability may become more evident as a child grows older. It often becomes more apparent with increased handwriting tasks. Poor eye-hand coordination may be noticeable as well as difficulty with visual-motor skills.

Chapter 7

ATTENTION DEFICIT DISORDERS

ATTENTION DEFICIT DISORDER DEFINED

John had meningitis as an infant and, like DJ, he faced some neurological challenges as a result. His parents became concerned when he was a toddler and displayed uncontrollable energy and impulsiveness. They sought help when, in their own words, "We just didn't like our own child." John's pediatrician diagnosed attention deficit disorder and tried several medications over the course of the next year. Once one was found that helped John calm down and focus, his parents said he was a changed child. John recently graduated from high school with honors.

Carla's impulsivity and her inability to connect consequences and actions were brought to her parents' attention by her first grade teacher. After a full evaluation by the IEP Team at her school, it was determined that Carla, too, had attention deficit disorder. Her parents were initially reluctant to try the recommended ritilin, but say it made a day and night difference in her school performance and in her ability to control her impulsivity. "Before the ritilin, we felt as if we were always yelling at our daughter. I dreaded the mornings and I cried every night," said Carla's mother.

Attention deficit disorder, also referred to as ADD, is characterized by a group of symptoms which are believed to be caused by slight abnormalities in the brain. These symptoms include difficulty in listening, focusing and following directions, impulsivity, clumsiness, and distractibility.

Attention deficit hyperactivity disorder (ADHD) is now considered a subcategory of ADD. The primary symptoms include a developmentally inappropriate lack of ability to attend, impulsivity, clumsiness, distractibility, and hyperactivity.

All cases of ADD are biological. Research has shown that ADD is a physiologically-based disorder with the brain functioning differently compared to normal cortical functioning.

There are several known causes for ADD. The disorder may result from disturbances in the biochemical processes of the brain. The difficulty initiates in the frontal area of the brain called the reticular activating system/locus ceruleus. This is known as the area that controls concentration, attention, and motivation. A decrease in blood flow to this area of the brain is associated with ADD. Other times there may be a deficiency of dopamine/norepinephrine or a decrease in blood flow to this part of the brain.

The second most common cause of ADD is alcohol or drug exposure in utero. As stated in the second chapter, even a minimal amount can result in serious consequences for the fetus.

ADD children generally have average intelligence, but frequently perform below ability. Learning disabilities (more recently referred to as perceptual and communication disorders) and ADD are two completely separate disorders; however, as many as 25 percent of children with ADD have a specific perceptual/communication disorder. ADD children generally do not perform well on standardized tests and testing may not be a reliable indicator of ability. Also, intelligence scores may decline over a period of time if the child has difficulty accumulating and assimilating academic knowledge.

ATTENTION DEFICIT DISORDER WITH HYPERACTIVITY

Characteristics of a child with ADHD may include the following: talks constantly; is restless and fidgety, often out of seat at school; touches, pokes, teases others around him or her; plays with any object within reach; has difficulty focusing and expressing one idea or thought at a time; is noisy, clumsy, and has poor coordination; is impulsive and does not easily handle delayed gratification; has poor self-regulatory behavior; does not follow home or classroom rules well; may have aggressive tendencies; is not interested in passive activities such as reading, listening to stories, or completing school work; and rapidly goes from one activity to another.

ADHD children tend to only be able to handle the length of time spent at any given activity as long as children who are two years younger up to 30 percent younger. Their emotional maturity is often up to three years lower than chronological age.

ATTENTION DEFICIT DISORDER WITHOUT HYPERACTIVITY

Children with ADD without hyperactivity may exhibit some of the following characteristics: more likely to be tense, nervous, remorseful and anxious; tend to more quiet and withdrawn; prefer to avoid confrontation; are passive; are easily confused; often have poor coordination and are clumsy; have a tendency toward daydreaming and often appear lost in thought; are much less fidgety and restless than ADHD children; and have tendencies toward being a loner.

ADD children have more difficulty getting focused whereas ADHD children cannot sustain attention. The nonhyperactive ADD child will generally have more problems in input, perceptual-motor speed, central cognitive processing speed and have inconsistent or poor memory retrieval. The ADHD child tends to have more difficulty in information output.

Both, ADD and ADHD children will demonstrate many of the following characteristics: have poor social skills; have problems in resolving disagreements and following generally accepted rules; are easily excitable; respond without thinking; have difficulty taking into consideration consequences of their own behavior and activities; have a tendency to blame others for mistakes; are impatient and easily frustrated; have difficulty waiting their turn; have many mood swings and often overreact; have difficulty handling change; have difficulty in appropriately expressing emotion; have trouble adjusting behavior to transition; have difficulty screening out distractions; often unable to understand and follow simple directions; and unable to stay on task–shifting from one uncompleted activity to another. In a school setting ADD and ADHD children demonstrate inconsistent academic and social performance; often have at least one other perceptual and communication disorder which affects academic achievement; have poor problem-solving skills; are constantly seeking additional help and have difficulty working alone; do not complete assignments; are disorganized and frequently lose homework and school materials; have a poor concept of time which affects their ability to use time effectively for completing assignments; and, the part of the brain which process-es reward/punishment concepts is impaired, so these children have a diminished sense of positive behavior reinforcement.

Even with modified educational planning which takes into consid-eration a child's ADD, the complications relative to the disorder are ongoing through adolescence and into adulthood. Currently, there is more movement toward positive reinforcement behavioral models, as opposed to punishment and negative reinforcement. Setting short-term behavior and academic goals appears to meet with more success.

ADD is a complex and often misunderstood disorder. It is widely diagnosed in a majority of foster and waiting children which is related to the number of children who have neurological special needs due to prenatal substance exposure and prematurity. On the positive side, there is a growing body of information and resources geared toward better understanding and management of ADD children. Once diag-nosed, most receive the support and help they need through their pediatricians and with their Individual Education Plan.

For parents who have questions about the possibility of ADD in their child, one of the best places to start is with the Special Education Department at your local school. Even a child as young as three can receive a full cost-free evaluation through the local school district. This also enables parents to locate early interventions services.

Chapter 8

INTELLECTUAL IMPAIRMENT

MENTAL RETARDATION

According to the American Psychiatric Association, there are three criteria for determining mental retardation:

1) Intellectual functioning must be significantly subaverage, which is defined as an IQ of 70 or below. Mild retardation falls within the IQ range of 50-70; moderate retardation falls within the range of 35-49; severe retardation falls between 20-30; and an IQ of below 20 is profound retardation.

2) The person is impaired in his or her ability to adapt to the environment.

3) Must become mentally retarded as a result of injury, disease, or a problem that existed before the age of 18. For example, if a young child suffered irreversible brain damage as the result of an accident, he would then be considered mentally retarded because it occurred during the developmental years. An adult who suffered the same consequences as the result of an accident would be considered to have organic brain damage because it occurred after the developmental years.

IQ TESTING AND SCORING

When trying to determine a child's IQ score, specific tests, which have been standardized for different age groups, are used.

The most commonly used tests are as follows:

Stanford-Binet Intelligence Scale
Riverside Publishing Co.
Chicago, 1986

For 2 years to 18 years. This is a norm-referenced intelligence test. It was revised in 1986 to provide scores in four subtest areas: verbal reasoning, abstract/visual reasoning, quantitative reasoning, and short term memory. A full-test composite score is provided as well.

Weshsler Preschool and Primary Scale of Intelligence (WPPSI)
The Psychological Corp.
New York, 1967
For 4 to 6 1/2 years. This is a norm-referenced general intelligence test. It provides a verbal IQ, and full scale IQ scores. It also gives a profile of strengths and weaknesses.

Weshsler Intelligence Scale for Children-Revised (WISC-R)
The Psychological Corp.
New York, 1967
For 6 years to 16 years/11 months. This is a norm-referenced general intelligence test. It provides scores for each subtest, a full-scale IQ score, performance IQ score, and verbal IQ score. Also provides a profile of strengths and weaknesses.

Weshsler Adult Intelligence Scale-Revised (WAIS-R)
The Psychological Corp.
New York, 1981
For 16 years and older. This is a norm-referenced general Intelligence test for adults. It provides a verbal IQ, performance IQ, full-scale IQ, and a profile of strengths and weaknesses.

McCarthy Scales of Children's Abilities
The Psychological Corp.
New York, 1972
For 2 1/2 years to 8 years. A norm-referenced test. It provides scores in the following five areas: verbal, perceptual performance, quantitative, memory, and motor. Also offer a general cognitive index for total test performance.

Kaufman Assessment Battery for Children (KABC)
American Guidance Services
Circle Pines, MN, 1983
For 2 1/2 years to 12 1/2 years. A norm-referenced intelligence test.

It is designed to assess learning potential and preferred learning style. Also provides scores scaled for mental processing subtests. Composite scores are available as well.

Mental and intelligence tests are the most frequently used psychological tests, though their validity and accuracy still remain controversial among professionals. However, most will agree that IQ tests do provide a cogent assessment of a person's thinking and problem-solving skills. The controversy arises when trying to determine what constitutes an appropriate measure of intelligence. The basic function of the IQ test is to provide a measurement of cognitive development. This includes: sensing; perceiving; differentiating one thing from another; remembering; recognizing; understanding pictures, words and numbers; developing concepts; judging; problem-solving; and reasoning.

An Intelligent Quotient, or IQ, is a test result expressed as a number that conveys how a child did on the test and how the performance of that child compares to what is expected for his or her specific age group. IQ scores are often related to other abilities of a child, particularly academic achievement.

In general, though, IQ tests and scores provide just one of many measures of the child's abilities. They can be helpful in planning needed educational or treatment services.

OTHER CAUSES OF MENTAL RETARDATION

Metabolic disorders in infants and children can often lead to mental retardation. One of the more common metabolic disorders is that of Tay-Sachs disease. This is a degenerative disease which results from an enzyme deficiency. Infants with Tay-Sachs appear normal at birth. However, within a short amount of time, they exhibit weak muscles, show failure to thrive, and develop blindness and severe mental retardation. These children usually die between 3 and 5 years of age.

Endocrine disorders, especially hypothyroidism, can be the cause of severe mental retardation if left undiagnosed and untreated. Hypothyroidism is caused by a lack of thyroid hormone or by the absence of a thyroid gland. In the United States, most infants are screened for endocrine disorders before leaving the hospital.

Other causes of mental retardation associated with birth include complications resulting from prematurity, severe bleeding during the birth process, serious brain infections, drug and alcohol exposure in utero, birth injury or lack of oxygen during delivery, infections during pregnancy, and malnutrition during brain development.

Causes of mental retardation after birth include accidents, injuries to the brain, infection, and trauma due to physical abuse.

In general, children with mild mental retardation (IQ 50-69) are independent within their families and community. They learn more slowly in school and may be limited in future vocational choices. They are capable of taking responsibility for their basic day-to-day needs. They are also capable of working and living independently as adults.

Moderately retarded (IQ 35-54) children can learn basic academic skills needed for semi-independent living. Their academic programs will generally focus on self-help skills, community living, and vocational training. They often are able to find employment within supervised work settings.

Severely mentally retarded (IQ 20-34) children generally have other disabilities such as speech and language problems, and motor difficulties. Educational programs will center around adaptive behavior, communication, and developmental skills. As adults, they can sometimes work in supervised workshop situations. Continued supervision is necessary all through adulthood.

Profoundly retarded (IQ 20-25) children often have many associated disabilities. However, some are able to learn basic self-care skills. Many are incapacitated by other problems such as hearing loss and visual and motor impairments.

BRAIN INJURY

Brain injury can occur for a variety of reasons. There can be a malformation during the development of the brain or there could be neurological damage to a child's developing brain.

Developmental brain malformation can result when something disrupts the brain's normal developmental process during the first or second trimester of pregnancy. For example, the baby's brain may not develop the required number of brain cells; brain cells may not migrate normally or where needed; or there may be a miscommunication between the brain cells during fetal development. Though the causes contributing to these malformations are not always known, they include genetic disorders, faulty blood supply to the brain (this is common with drug or alcohol exposed infants), or chromosome abnormalities with too little or too much genetic material.

Neurological impairment can occur when there is an injury to the brain either before, during, or after birth. The most common causes of injury are related to premature birth. Also included are significantly difficult delivery, neonatal medical complications, or some type of trauma to the brain. These can be preceded by lack of oxygen before, during, or after birth; bleeding in the brain; trauma to the head such as a fall, car accident, or birth injury; metabolic disorders such as low glucose levels, or severe jaundice; infection to the nervous system such as encephalitis or meningitis; or toxic impairment such as that which occurs from alcohol or drug use by a birth parent during pregnancy.

BORDERLINE INTELLECTUAL FUNCTIONING

Borderline intellectual functioning is the category used when a child has an IQ in the 71-84 range. These are children who appear to be lower functioning intellectually, but their IQs are above the 70 range used to diagnose mental retardation.

This is a difficult category to diagnose because of possible differentiating factors including cultural, social, or environmental. It is also hard to differentiate between borderline intellectual functioning and mental retardation when other mental or medical conditions have been diagnosed.

Chapter 9

PERVASIVE DEVELOPMENTAL DISORDERS

PERVASIVE DEVELOPMENTAL DISORDERS DEFINED

For almost ten years, Jack's parents struggled to understand their son who once showed such promise as a toddler. They tried to determine if he was gifted, difficult, or overly emotional. His temper tantrums were beyond what they had experienced with their other children. He did not socialize, even with his own siblings. One of his teachers informed his parents that he was spoiled and bratty. After a decade of therapists, misinformation, and unsolicited advice, they finally found a physician who diagnosed Asperger's syndrome, a pervasive developmental disorder akin to autism. Like autism, Asperger's is caused by a neurological abnormality.

One of the more well-known autistic individuals is Temple Grandin, a Colorado State University professor of animal science. Her design of livestock control systems is known worldwide. However, the majority of people with pervasive developmental disorders will not be able to function independently. There are advances being made in earlier diagnosis of autism. Until about seven years ago have experts been able to diagnose this and related disorders as early as age two. The earlier a child is diagnosed, the sooner he or she can receive positive intervention. At the University of Washington's Experimental Unit, there is in increase of an average 20 points in the IQs of children who begin the early intervention program between the ages of two to four. This, in turn, affords them the opportunity to succeed in regular classrooms later.

Pervasive developmental disorders in children are characterized by a profound disturbance in socialization, impairment in the areas of verbal and nonverbal communication, and poor imagination and empathy. There is a lack of peer relationships and inappropriate cling-ing. Children with pervasive developmental disorder often exhibit excessive anxiety, are extremely resistant to change, demonstrate motor movement oddities such as excessive spinning, may have speech abnormalities, and are often hyper- or hyposensitive to acts of self-injury and sensory stimuli. These children are incapable of func-tioning independently and will always require supervision and special educational facilities. Childhood onset pervasive developmental dis-order is the diagnosis given if these symptoms appear after 30 months of age and before the age of 12.

AUTISM

Autism is a physical impairment of the brain which results in a life-long developmental disability. Autism can manifest itself through many different symptoms, which can occur by themselves or in com-bination with other disorders such as seizures, mental retardation, or sensory impairments. Symptoms may appear differently in different children. Many autistic children exhibit what is known as stereotyped behavior, which is a repetitive behavior. Though often bizarre, this stereotyped behavior varies greatly from child to child.

There are six major symptoms of autism. The first is an inability to develop normal socialization. Children with autism appear to be extremely isolated. They act uninterested in other people. They are unable to attach to others and usually express little or no emotion. They often avoid any type of eye contact. Many autistic children will arch their backs or stiffen when a loved one attempts to hold or cud-dle them. They have limited social skills and are unable to relate to the world outside of themselves. This inability to socialize is usually the first indicator of autism.

Another symptom of autistic behavior is abnormal relationships to events or objects. Autistic children have a great need for day-to-day consistency. They become upset and disoriented if their schedule is changed or their environment is altered. Children with autism gener-ally use toys or other objects in what is considered "nonfunctional ways." They may participate in repetitive activities with their toys, activities which have no meaning to others.

Autistic children often exhibit atypical responses to sensory stimuli. They tend to either completely overreact to any type of sensory stimulation, or they may have no reaction whatsoever. It is not unusual for an autistic child to appear hearing impaired because of his or her inability to react to sounds and commotion around himself or herself. Most autistic children will use their sense of taste and smell much more often than their sense of sight or hearing. Autistic children often respond to motion in irregular ways. They may be able to spin incessantly without ever appearing dizzy or off-balance.

Irregularities in language, speech, and other types of communication may be an indicator of autism. About 40 percent of children diagnosed with autism do not speak at all. Others may only parrot what is said to them. This is called echolalia. This may involve repeating songs or commercials, or it may manifest itself in the repeating of a sentence by a parent or a loved one.

Another symptom of autism involves developmental delays. However, this one is not as easy to gauge, as most children vary in their development and are still considered within normal limits. Also, an autistic child may appear to develop normally up to about age two to three, and then many of the gains he or she has made seem to disappear.

Lastly, autism will initially manifest itself during early childhood or infancy. It is not unusual for an autistic child to be diagnosed with mental retardation without autism even considered as a secondary diagnosis. This is because 80 percent of the children with autism are also mentally retarded. Generally speaking, though, autism is diagnosed before the child is three years of age. And, irregardless of the age of diagnosis, children with autism will almost always exhibit symptoms in the other five categories.

In the United States, there are approximately 360,000 people diagnosed with autism. This figure includes the 110,000 cases of full-syndrome autism, and 250,000 people who exhibit most of the symptoms. For unknown reasons, autism occurs about four times more frequently in boys than in girls. However, when girls are affected, they are more likely to have lower IQs and are often more seriously disabled.

CAUSES OF AUTISM

It is not yet known why some children have autism. Doctors and scientists do not completely understand the cause of autism or how it affects the brain structure. At this time the only genetic connection with autism is a condition called Fragile-X syndrome. As stated in the previous chapter, Fragile-X is a genetically-inherited form of mental retardation.

A child's autism is most likely the result of a combination of biochemical and neurological disorders from birth. Children with autism will display a wide range of abilities. The child with a less severe form of autism will probably have fewer disabilities as an adult. A few children with autism even reach normal functioning as adults. However, most will continue to be largely affected by their autism throughout adulthood and will require supervision on a continuing basis all of their lives. Autistic children with an IQ level within the 60-70 range tend to have a more positive long-term prognosis. Other contributing factors include early intervention programs and/or positive experiences in a mainstreamed school setting.

Autism has attracted closer scrutiny and study in recent years. The end result is the increase of more educational and vocational programs for autistic children and adults. With parental involvement, increasing community acceptance and integration, autistic people have a much greater opportunity for growth and accomplishment. The Appendix lists resources for those who live with and work with autistic children and adults.

OTHER PERVASIVE DEVELOPMENTAL DISORDERS

There are several other pervasive developmental disorders which are not seen as often as autism. These are Rett's disorder, childhood disintegrative disorder, and Asperger's disorder. Rett's disorder is characterized by a loss of previously acquired skills between ages 5 and 30 months. These children have a normal prenatal and perinatal experience. They have normal psychomotor development through at least the first five months of life. At birth their head circumference is within normal parameters. Between 5 and 48 months, there is a deceleration of head growth. There is also the loss of purposeful hand skills along with the development of stereotyped hand movements such as hand wringing. After the first few years of onset, the child begins to lose interest in the social environment. However, newly learned social interaction can take place. There are problems with coordination and full body movement as well as severe psychomotor deficits. This disorder is most often associated with severe or profound mental retardation.

In childhood disintegrative disorder, there is a significant regression in several areas of functioning after a period of at least two years of normal growth and development in the areas of communication, social interaction, play, and other behaviors. Between the ages of two and ten, the child begins to rapidly lose previously acquired skills in a number of areas including social skills, adaptive behavior, expressive or receptive language, motor skills, play, and bowel or bladder control. There is marked impairment in social interaction and stereotyped patterns of activity and behavior. This disorder is sometimes referred to as Heller's syndrome and is most often associated with severe mental retardation.

Asperger's disorder is characterized by severe and continued impairment in social interaction with the development of repetitive and restricted patterns of behavior and activity. There are marked deficits in social and occupational areas of functioning. However, there are no significant language delays and cognitive development is generally on target. This disorder is often not recognized as such until preschool when the lack of social interaction is noticed. There is often an absence of social or emotional reciprocity and an inability to share interests or enjoyment with others. Also, this child is unable to develop peer relationships and there is usually a great deal of motor clumsiness.

All three of these pervasive developmental disorders are almost always of lifelong duration.

Chapter 10

MOVEMENT DISORDERS

TRANSIENT TIC DISORDER

A tic is defined as a repetitive, uncontrolled movement of a muscle or small muscle group caused by muscle contraction. Most often, tic occurs in the facial, shoulder, or arm muscles. In transient tic disorder, the identifying characteristics are involuntary, recurrent, repetitive, and rapid movements. These movements can be voluntarily suppressed for several minutes up to several hours. Tics disappear during sleep but may be more noticeable during periods of tension and stress.

The most common tic is an eye blink or another facial tic, but they can involve larger muscle groups. A transient tic will last at least one month but no longer than one year.

CHRONIC MOTOR TIC DISORDER

Chronic tics are characterized by recurrent, involuntary, repetitive, rapid movements. In general, chronic tics will not involve more than three muscle groups at a time. These movements can be voluntarily suppressed for several minutes up to several hours at a time. The duration of a chronic motor tic is at least one year, and the intensity of the symptoms is consistent over several weeks or months at a time. A chronic motor tic can present vocally in the form of grunts or other low noises caused by muscle contractions in the abdomen, chest, or diaphragm.

TOURETTE'S DISORDER

The identifying features include involuntary, recurrent, repetitive, rapid movements, including multiple vocal tics. The vocal tics present as grunts, clicks, yelps, barks, sniffs, or coughs. Infrequently (less than 10 percent), the vocalizations involve an irresistible urge to repeat obscenities. This is referred to as coprolalia. The more complex motor tics in Tourette's involve movements such as deep knee bends, touching, twirling, or retracing steps. The onset of this disorder is before 18 years of age and the first symptoms often involve throat clearing, stuttering, hopping and skipping, sniffing, tongue protrusion, and sniffing. All of these symptoms disappear with sleep, but they worsen with stress and tension. Tourette's can be voluntarily suppressed for awhile, but the symptoms almost always reappear. It is not uncommon for children with Tourette's to have accompanying disorders such as Obsessive-Compulsive Disorder, Attention Deficit/Hyperactivity Disorder, or Learning Disorders. These children may also have problems with depression because of the social discomfort and self-consciousness associated with Tourette's. In the more severe forms, Tourette's can interfere with basic daily activities. Tourette's is usually a lifelong disorder, though there may be periods of remission for a period of weeks up to several years. In many cases, the severity of the symptoms begins to taper off during early adolescence and continue to abate through adulthood. In rare instances, the symptoms disappear altogether by early adulthood.

STEREOTYPED MOVEMENT DISORDER

Stereotyped movement disorder refers to rocking, repetitive hand or arm movements, or head banging. This disorder is much more prevalent in children with mental retardation or among children who have little to no social stimulation, like many of the Romanian orphans in recent years. This disorder, unlike tics, is voluntary.

Chapter 11

EATING DISORDERS

Judy has struggled with weight problems all of her life. She recalls feeling left out when it came to school and social activities. "People would look at me, but they wouldn't see me; they just saw my weight," she told me. Her battle with bulimia began in high school. She would take up to twenty laxatives at a time in order to purge her body of the food she had previously eaten. She would gag herself with the handle of a spoon to induce vomiting. Her weight continued to roller coaster and her health suffered. Eventually she was hospitalized and it was at this time that she met a therapist who helped her change her negative patterns of behavior. Today she lives a much healthier lifestyle without dieting or binges, and she is herself now a parent. Judy is one of the success stories in our weight conscious society. Unfortunately, many children learn at an early age that body image seems to take precedence over so many other aspects of life. Although no age is immune, eating disorders are especially prevalent in teenagers and young adults.

ANOREXIA NERVOSA

The primary identifying feature of anorexia nervosa is an intense fear of becoming obese. Related symptoms include significant weight loss, refusal to maintain normal body weight, and disturbance of body image. This disorder is predominant in females. The child with this disorder speaks of feeling fat when they are range from normal to severely underweight.

They are usually preoccupied with looking at themselves in the mirror. These youngsters will lose at least 25 percent of their body weight.

This is usually done through excessive exercise, self-induced vomiting, the use of diuretics or laxatives, and a strict reduction of food intake. In latter stages, there can be hypothermia, bradycardia, hypotension, metabolic changes, and the appearance of lanugo.

Preteens or teenagers with anorexia have a very distorted view of their body. They either feel generally overweight or they become increasingly obsessed with a specific part of their body, such as the thighs, the buttocks, or abdomen. These children will often use a wide range of techniques to figure their size or weight. These include excessive weighing, obsessive measuring, and use of a mirror. Their self-esteem and general confidence is based on their perceived body shape and weight.

An adolescent with this disorder can experience a delay in psychosexual development. Most youths with anorexia are resistant to treatment and adamantly deny there is a problem. Anorexia nervosa occurs most frequently in late adolescents, although it is not uncommon to see it as early as puberty.

Anorexia is often accompanied by depression, social withdrawal, irritability, and the inability to sleep.

BULIMIA

Bulimia is characterized by episodes of binge eating, the fear of not being able to stop the binge, and depressed mood after the food binge. The binges are often planned and are hidden from others. The food is generally high in fat and calories with a sweet taste. The food is eaten quickly with little chewing. Many with this disorder end the binge with induced vomiting to relieve the physical discomfort and the guilt that often accompanies these eating binges. Others misuse laxatives as a compensatory method to prevent weight gain. Like anorexia, children with bulimia base much of their self-worth on their perceived impression of their body and weight. To be clinically diagnosed with bulimia, a child would binge eat and use the compensatory method of relief a minimum of twice a week for three months.

Youths with this disorder often have frequent fluctuations in weight greater than 10 pounds. Bulimia is seen most often in late adolescence. These youths are generally ashamed of their eating problems and seek to hide the symptoms. Binges can be preceded by depression, stress, or hunger following strict dieting. The binge is often followed by more depression and low self-worth. Some youths will fast for several days and exercise excessively after a binge. This relieves the fear of weight gain and gives the individual a sense of regaining the control lost to the binge.

PICA

Pica is characterized by the persistent eating of nonfood substances. These include, but are not limited to, dirt, hair, chalk, paint, plaster, string, sand, bugs, animal droppings, leaves, and pebbles. This disorder usually shows up around the age of two but often disappears by early childhood. Pica can be the result of a mineral deficiency and it is not uncommon to see it in children who are mentally retarded.

OTHER EATING DISORDERS OF INFANCY OR EARLY CHILDHOOD

The other two known eating disorders associated with infants or children are rumination disorder and feeding disorder of infancy or early childhood. Although rare in the United States, it is not uncommon to see these disorders as a result of the overcrowded and under-staffed conditions of orphanages in other countries.

Rumination disorder is characterized by repeated regurgitation and rechewing of food. This disorder generally appears in an infant or child after a period of normal development. The regurgitation is not a result of any gastrointestinal difficulties or other medical conditions. There is no nausea or gag when the food is brought up. Rumination is seen most often in infants; however, it is not uncommon in older children if associated with severe mental retardation.

Infants with this disorder are usually irritable and hungry between bouts or regurgitation. Rumination often leads to malnutrition and failure to thrive because the infant is unable to keep enough ingested food down in order to gain weight. There is also a mortality rate estimated as high as 25 percent. Predisposing features to rumination disorder include extreme neglect and little or no stimulation, stressful life, and difficulties in the primary caregiver/child relationship.

Feeding disorder of infancy or early childhood is characterized by the inability to eat enough in order to gain weight, or by continued weight loss over the period of at least a month. Infants with this disorder act irritable and are not easily consoled even during or immediately after a feeding. They are often developmentally delayed because of a failure to thrive. This condition can be the result of extreme neglect or abuse, neuroregulatory difficulties, or other developmental disabilities which might make the infant less responsive.

Chapter 12

AFFECTIVE DISORDERS

Patty's parents describe their daughter as being extremely emotional from the moment she was born. They recall spending hours trying to get her to sleep. As a toddler, she exhibited overwhelming fear when she left her home; she would not even venture onto the playground equipment at a nearby park. She would physically cling to her mother anytime they were out in public and she was inconsolable, even in the briefest of periods, when her parents were not in sight. She had extreme tantrums all through preschool and she was often hysterical. She also exhibited an unusual preoccupation with death; it was often the topic of her school essays. At the urging of one of her elementary school teachers, Patty's parents took her to see a psychiatrist who diagnosed manic-depressive illness, also known as bipolar disorder. Patty's parents decided not to try the recommended medications at that time because of the possible side effects. It was not until Patty attempted suicide as a teenager that they sought medical intervention. There were no quick fixes and it took several combinations of medications to find the most workable solution for Patty. She still has days when she is manic or depressed, but the duration is shorter and more controllable. She is now an honor student with a bright outlook and hope for her future.

SEPARATION ANXIETY DISORDER

Separation anxiety disorder is characterized by excessive worry on being separated from primary attachment figures or from home. These children often feel anxiety to the point of becoming panicked. The reaction goes beyond the expectation for that child's developmental stage. Children with this disorder do not like to visit or sleep over at the homes of friends and are frequently afraid to go to school, camping, or on other outings. They are often clingy with a parent and have frequent physical complaints of headaches and stomachaches. When separated from loved ones, these children are often preoccupied with illness or death befalling themselves or their parents.

Another common feature is a fear of going to sleep. These children will not go to bed without a parent near them. Nightmares are common as a result of the child's morbid preoccupation with death and other fears. Other children may not experience as much fear; rather, they become acutely homesick and are unable to participate in any other activity save daydreaming about the return to home and family.

Separation anxiety disorder is often the result of a traumatic event such as the death of a close relative or pet, a serious illness, or a move to a new area. It can occur in children as young as preschool age, but the extreme forms of the disorder are more often seen around the age of ten or eleven. This disorder can run from a couple of weeks to several years. It may precede the adult disorder of agoraphobia. These children are usually compliant and eager to please, though they may physically strike out at anyone trying to separate them from their caregiver or home. It is not uncommon for this disorder to be accompanied by increasing depressive mood disorders. Older children and young adults may develop an inability to function outside the home, limiting moving, getting married, or handling a job.

AVOIDANT DISORDER

This disorder features a persistent and excessive fear of strangers. These children still express a clear desire for affection from family, friends, and other loved ones. But the fear of strangers is so intense, these kids often avoid many social functions with peers. Children with this disorder may cling and whisper to their parents, but become extremely anxious, and often tearful when expected to speak to someone unfamiliar. These children often lack self-confidence and are unassertive. In adolescence, their psychosexual development may be delayed or inhibited. Younger children may come across as slow and inarticulate, although there are no perceptual and communication disorders associated with avoidant disorder. This disorder is rarely seen past early adolescence. However, those individuals who go on to develop avoidant personality disorder have very restricted interpersonal contacts, are hypersensitive, and have difficulty maintaining or advancing in employment. If this impairment continues into adulthood, it is not uncommon for an additional diagnoses of dependent personality disorder because these individuals become extremely dependent and attached to only a handful of people.

OVERANXIOUS DISORDER

Overanxious disorder is characterized by excessive worry that is not based on a specific fear. Also, it does not follow any known psychosocial stressor. The youth with this disorder may be overly concerned about what others will think of him or her, injury, future events, performance on schoolwork, etc. These children are frequently perfectionist and obsessive with feelings of self-doubt. Also noticeable is the persistent seeking of approval. This disorder is seen most often in eldest children, smaller families, upper socioeconomic groups, and within families where there is persistent emphasis on performance.

CHILDHOOD DEPRESSIONS

Recent studies have shown that mood disorders, which affect the emotional balance of a person, are a result of a biochemical imbalance. It is strongly believed by many mental health professionals that there is a genetic predisposition for many of the known depressions.

Bipolar affective disorder is also referred to as a manic/depression is not a common depression in children but it does occur. A child with bipolar affective disorder suffers episodes of depression followed by a period of mania, or extreme elation. These are interspersed with periods of normal feelings. The length, duration, and number of these mood swings differ from person to person.

In bipolar affective disorder, when a child is in the depressed state, he or she may feel unable to function at all. These children sleep often and do not want to get out of bed. When they do arise, they move slowly. Schoolwork suffers and self-esteem is extremely poor. Children, even young ones, who are in this state of depression, may be suicidal. In the manic state, a child feels as if there are no problems that cannot be conquered. There are no barriers to what he or she wants. These children get little sleep, speak rapidly, and laugh continuously. They may go on spending sprees.

Bipolar affective disorder is usually treated with mood regulators such as lithium, in combination with psychotherapy. Often, medication to supplement the effects of the mood regulator is also needed. This is often a lifelong condition.

Major depression is more often referred to as clinical or severe depression. It is recurrent, long-lasting, and life threatening. One of the things that professional therapists are discovering in recent years is that depression in children happens as frequently and as severely as the depression suffered by adults. Children are more apt to hide their depression with other behaviors that are misdiagnosed as oppositional, hyperactive, learning disabled, or lazy. Misunderstood and untreated clinical depression leaves a child vulnerable to suicide attempts.

In order for a child to be diagnosed with a major depressive disorder, he or she must have five of the following nine symptoms for a duration of at least two weeks:

1. Takes no pleasure from and no longer participates in favorite activities.
2. Acts irritable and depressed most of the time.
3. Has lost or gained more than 5 percent of his or her body weight, or has not had expected weight gain for age.
4. Acts extremely restless or extremely lethargic.
5. Is either unable to sleep or sleeps all of the time.
6. Acts tired most of the time.
7. Experiences excessive guilt feelings or feelings of worthlessness most of the time.
8. Is unable to concentrate or make decisions.
9. Has no other physical illness that precipitated the depression, and has not suffered the loss of a loved one.

Treatment of clinical depression usually requires initial hospitalization, followed by a combination of psychotherapy and drug therapy. Lithium is often used to stabilize brain function and other medications are used for the depressive episodes. Psychotherapy helps to give the child new skills and strategies in managing the illness. Exercise is also encouraged as a natural way to help regulate mood.

Chapter 13

BEHAVIORAL DISORDERS

Kayron is a young girl who has experienced many losses in a short period of time. She was removed from her birth family due to physical, sexual, and emotional abuse. She has experienced multiple foster placements and was considered unmanageable because of her oppositional behaviors. She was moved to a therapeutic residential facility, but her overall behavior is still quite inconsistent. In Kayron's situation, it is likely that her oppositional behaviors are a result of her attachment issues. Attachment disorders, as they relate to foster care and adoption, are dealt with more thoroughly later in this chapter. Behavioral disorders, however, are not strictly an adoptive issue—perhaps we are just better able to identify them in the arena of foster care because these children generally come with such an extensive social history.

Joe, on the other hand, appeared to be a fairly typical child, reaching all early developmental milestones. By second grade, he began to struggle more noticeably with his schoolwork. He was diagnosed with a reading disorder. He began to experience some depression and behavioral problems. His aggression increased until he was placed in a special education setting for children with behavioral disorders. With therapy and medication, his social skills have improved dramatically and he is learning how to control his behavior and impulsivity.

CONDUCT DISORDERS

Conduct disorders are characterized by a way of acting which shows little to no regard for the rights of others, and an absence of concern for rules or societal expectations. Other features of conduct disorders include: difficulties at home and at school; precocious sexual activity; a tendency to blame others; mistrust of others; feelings of being unfairly treated; low self-esteem and poor self-image; engaging in early age drinking, smoking, or other substance use; frequent outbursts of temper; frequent irritability with a low tolerance level; and underachievement academically. It is not uncommon for conduct disorders to be secondary to attention deficit disorder, or another specific developmental disorder.

This impairment ranges in degree from mild to severe. Residential treatment may be necessary for those youths who exhibit antisocial behavior.

Other predisposing factors include: parental rejection frequent changing of parent figures (foster parents, residential treatment facilities, relatives); alcohol dependent parent figures; and harsh discipline with inconsistent nurturing.

In the more severe forms, this disorder may manifest itself in physical violence against others, including acts of vandalism, rape, fire-setting, and assault. Children with a conduct disorder often initiate aggressive behavior and react aggressively toward others. They repeatedly act in a threatening and intimidating manner. They initiate frequent physical fights and they generally employ the use of weapons in these confrontations. Deliberate fire-setting with the express intent to cause damage and harm is a common feature of conduct disorder, as is cruelty to people and animals. On the less serious end of the spectrum, the behaviors might include persistent truancy, running away, telling serious lies, stealing without confrontation of the victim, and substance abuse. Children who are diagnosed with a conduct disorder with onset prior to ten years of age are morel likely to develop the adult disorder of antisocial personality.

OPPOSITIONAL DEFIANT DISORDER

The primary feature of this disorder is a persistent pattern of negativity and provocative opposition toward authority figures. Most often, the attitude of opposition is directed toward family members and teachers. Other characteristics include violating minor rules, frequent temper tantrums, argumentativeness, stubbornness, and actively defying or refusing to comply with any boundaries set forth by an adult. This child will frequently do things to deliberately annoy others. Defiant behaviors include persistent stubborness, refusal to follow directions, and an unwillingness to compromise or negotiate with adults or peers. There is a marked testing of limits which is displayed by ignoring orders and failing to accept any blame for misbehaviors.

Oppositional disorder is differentiated from the conduct disorders in that there is no violation of basic rights of others or of age-appropriate, societal expectations. Children with this disorder usually blame others for the problem and they do not view themselves as oppositional. School and family difficulties are not uncommon. Usually this disorder begins in late childhood or early adolescence. It is frequently chronic and lasts for several years. It often interferes with all social relationships.

Oppositional defiant disorder is prevalent in children who have disrupted home or family situations as is so often seen in foster and residential care. It is also common in families where there is harsh and inconsistent discipline or neglectful parenting. Attention deficit/hyperactivity disorder, and learning or communication disorders are frequently seen in children with oppositional defiant disorder.

ATTACHMENT DISORDERS

Many mental healthcare professionals feel that attachment disorder is one of the primary causes of rapidly increasing and violent crime in the U.S. Nonattachment is characterized by the incapacity of the child to form any human bonds; remoteness; lack of emotion and connection with others; superficial engaging; lack of eye contact; indiscriminate affection; destructive behaviors toward self, others, and property; cruelty to animals; lack of impulse control; lack of cause and effect thinking; lack of conscience; abnormal eating patterns; poor peer relationships; preoccupation with fire; incessant chatter and persistent nonsense questioning; inappropriate demands and clinginess; and abnormal speech patterns.

Attachment problems can be associated with developmental delays, feeding disorder of infancy or early childhood, pica, or rumination disorder. Attachment disorder is differentiated from other disorders such as mental retardation and pervasive developmental disorder in that the difficulties are a direct result of gross pathological care. These include a persistent disregard of the child's basic emotional needs for stimulation and nurturing, a continued neglect of the child's physical needs, or frequent changes in the child's primary caregiver, abuse, neglect, and child-caregiver relational difficulties. Malnutrition can also be a contributing factor.

Attachment disorders are a primary concern in adoption. Children generally have attachment problems when their attachment cycle is interrupted within the first couple years of life. Attachment disorders worsen with repeated moves through the foster system and with disrupted adoptions.

Therapy for nonattached children often includes intense sessions which require whole family participation. Attachment challenges, as they relate to adoptive situations are discussed in Chapter 15.

Chapter 14

EDUCATION AND CHILDREN WITH SPECIAL NEEDS

INDIVIDUALS WITH DISABILITIES EDUCATION ACT (IDEA)

The third statute of the IDEA is Public Law 94–142, the Education for All Handicapped Children Act of 1975. This is the law that set the precedent for federal special education legislation. It is significant in that it was the statute that made parents and other caregivers the primary educational advocate for their child. Now parents have the means to act in their child's best educational interest. Before this Act, parents of severely disabled children were often told that the school districts simply could not provide educational services for their child. In P.L. 94–142, special education is specifically defined as "specially designed instruction designed to meet the unique needs of a child with disabilities." This designed instruction is referred to as an Individualized Education Plan or IEP.

There are six major provisions of P.L. 94–142. They are as follows:

1. The education for children with disabilities means that all children, no matter the severity of the disability, can receive educational services. As of 1990, all states are required to provide services for children ages three through eighteen. Most states actually provide services for children ages birth through twenty-one.

2. Children will be tested fairly to determine if they will receive services. Before a child is eligible to receive special education or learning disabled services, he or she must be tested and evaluated by a team of professionals. These tests must demonstrate a child's strengths and weaknesses. This is referred to as nondiscriminatory testing. Another requirement is that the tests be given to children in their own language and in such a manner that their abilities and disabilities are accurately

featured. Children are eligible for special education services based on several tests and evaluations instead of a single test score.

3. Schools have a duty to provide individually designed, appropriate programs for every child at no cost to their parents. P.L. 94–142 ensures that all children eligible for special services will receive a free and appropriate education. This also means that, even if a child has to receive his or her educational services in a private or residential facility, the state and local school systems must bear the financial responsibility. "Appropriate education" is to be determined by parents and other educational professionals. Again, this is a part of the IEP process. For a child under the age of three, this plan is referred to as the Individualized Family Services Plan. In this case, many of the professionals working with the family may be employed by the health department or other social service departments. The IFSP will provide early intervention services for these families. It may include family counseling or training, services such as speech or occupational therapies, and support group help.

Both the IEP and IFSP may include such services as speech/language therapy, occupational or physical therapy, special transportation services; individual or family counseling, and any other services necessary to enable a child to benefit from an appropriate education.

4. Children with disabilities will be educated with children who are nondisabled. Prior to 1975, children with disabilities were segregated from nondisabled children. Currently, the federal law mandates that all students have equal access to educational services. The result was most immediately noticed with "mainstreaming." This means that more specially challenged children were integrated into their neighborhood schools. P.L. 94–142 has enabled students who are eligible for special services to be educated in the "least restrictive environment. Whenever an IEP is written, parents and educators decide how much time a child with disabilities will spend in a typical classroom, in other school activities and in special education instruction. Only a student whose disabilities are of such a severe nature that it would be impossible to provide instruction in a typical classroom will be educated in a separate classroom or school.

5. Decisions made by the school system can be challenged by the parents or other legal caregivers. Prior to P.L. 94–142, parents were allowed minimal input as to the educational decisions made by the school system. Under P.L. 94–142, parents and students have a right

to "due process." Parents are able to call for the services of an impartial third party in order to solve disputes between the other IEP team members and parents. Parents can challenge decisions made in the areas of inclusion or exclusion from special educational services, nondiscriminatory testing, the appropriateness of educational services, the placement of a child in least restrictive environment, and other related services. In addition to the right to challenge decisions in these areas, parents have a right to "notice," meaning that before any change can be made in regard to a child's IEP, a parent must be notified. This includes testing, entering or exiting special education services, time previously determined in a typical classroom and in special education instruction, and other changes. In most cases, these changes will require a parent's written consent after notification.

6. Parents of children with disabilities will actively participate in the decision-making process and planning for their child's special education. This means that parents and other custodial caregivers are encouraged to take an active roll—an advocacy roll in the education of their child. These are the people who know and understand a child best. Parents understanding, their expectations, experiences, and vision for their child will be in active partnership with the professional IEP team.

I have been involved in planning and implementing IEP's for three of my children, and I have found it to be an extremely positive and rewarding experience. I have been fortunate to find team members who are thoughtful and receptive to my husband's and my insights into our children. I have heard from other parents who did not feel so fortunate, who considered the IEP process intimidating and incomprehensible. It really should never work this way. It has been my experience that when a parent approaches the process positively and with the understanding that the IEP team is there to help, the relationship becomes reciprocal. We parents can be, understandably, defensive about our children's rights. However, I have yet to meet an educator who, when I expressed fears of misunderstanding my child's special needs, did not respond helpfully and positively.

Another resource I have found extremely helpful is that of the school psychologist and social worker. The following section has been written by the psychologist who helped our family with the transition of an older child placement. She and the school social worker were very understanding in the areas of attachment and family bonding as associated with older child foster and adoptive care.

THE ROLE OF THE SCHOOL PSYCHOLOGIST
AND SOCIAL WORKER

By Barbara Shedore, Psy. D.

For a parent or guardian, the school psychologist and social worker can be valuable resources. The school psychologist and social worker work together and sometimes their duties overlap. A psychologist has a doctoral degree and is trained to give intelligence and other psychological tests. A social worker has a master's degree, and is often the family's liaison, with the educational system and other community systems (providing home visits, if desired). Both offer assessments of a child's social or emotional needs and skills, consult with teachers and staff members, and work with families on how best to support their children. Sometimes they provide individual or group counseling.

Every school, including preschool and kindergarten, has a psychologist and social worker available. Often, their initial involvement is a result of concerns from a parent or teacher. For example, a parent may share with a teacher some questions about the educational or social progress of their child. Or they may feel concerned about a child's level of stress due to family issues or recent experiences. They may feel, for whatever reason, that their child could be performing at a higher level, or have reservations about their child's behavior. The teacher, the parent or both may decide to contact the school psychologist as an additional resource. Other educators are familiar with how to access the services of the psychologist or social worker. Or, a parent can call the school or district directly and schedule an appointment. The school psychologist and social worker want to help a child get the most from their classroom education. If children are worried or troubled, they may have a difficult time concentrating. Kids can appear to be daydreaming when they are actually anxious, worried, or depressed. Other children will express their problems by acting-out or getting into trouble; they may demonstrate oppositional or other defiant behaviors. Schools try to work with families on helping to keep the child's problems and worries from interfering with their learning. The mental health team teaches social skills, so that children can improve their relationships with other children and adults, and better learn how to resolve conflict. The psychologist and social worker work as a team with other staff members on understanding a child and how to provide that child with the support needed in each individual case.

They may consult with staff or parents on behavior management. Children often express their feelings with acting-out behavior unless taught other coping skills.

Psychologists and social workers may provide counseling during school hours. They offer groups on a particular social skill or work with children who have similar needs. For example, children whose parents are divorcing may share feelings in common and be joined in a support group. Other examples include children who have trouble controlling their temper or are impulsive, or children who have experienced a trauma. All of these and other situations may receive help through group therapy with mental health professionals. Individual counseling is also available, with parental permission, or a family may receive referral help to other professionals. For children with long-term issues or needing more specialized services, the psychologist or social worker may suggest more intensive intervention by referring to an outside agency or psychotherapist. These professionals may be helpful with other diagnoses related to ADD, depression, or trauma.

For children receiving special education services, the psychologist and social worker participate with other team members in staffings and writing a child's IEP (Individual Education Plan). They are only part of an entire team effort which includes parents, educators, and other school professionals.

The IEP will document a child's strengths and needs, as well as other areas where additional support is warranted. The plan includes concrete, measurable goals, plus broader objectives aimed at all of their needs. Many different school specialists participate in assessing a child's strengths and challenges. Often, the school psychologist is involved in assessing a child's cognitive abilities through an IQ test or other psychological tests. Sometimes an IQ test is given to rule out problems in this area or give more information to the total picture of a child. The school then implements the plan and continues to monitor progress and changes needed in the follow-up process.

Psychologists and social workers are trained to use a nonjudgmental approach for children and their families. They try to be helpful without being accusatory. They are employees of the school district, and therefore completely separate from social services or the health department—the agencies responsible for investigating abuse and neglect. Like all school personnel, they must report suspected abuse when a suspicion arises.

Mental health teams support children both academically and socially. It is difficult for an unhappy child to concentrate, or benefit from class when he or she cannot get along with peers and adults. When a child has experienced upsetting life events, it is normal to react in many unusual or unexpected ways, unless given helpful new ways of coping with their pain. These children deserve as much support as possible. Schools and families working together is the most helpful and effective approach. When parents and schools work together, the children benefit.

The next section is written by a teacher of many years who has specialized in working with gifted and talented children. Children recognized as gifted and talented often present their own unique set of special needs or challenges.

THE SPECIAL NEEDS OF GIFTED AND TALENTED CHILDREN

By Diane Strevey

Another group of children, not commonly thought of to have special needs, are the gifted and talented. In 1972, the US Office of Education declared, "Gifted and talented children are those identified by professionally qualified persons who by virtue of outstanding abilities are capable of high performance. They are children who require differentiated educational programs and/or services beyond those normally provided by the regular school programs in order to realize areas of their contribution to self and society." In many states, gifted and talented children are included in the legal definition of exceptional children. Disabilities or language differences characterize other exceptional students. Precocious intellectual ability and strong potential for extraordinary performance are defining properties of gifted and talented children. There are varying characteristics of gifted and talented children which should be recognized and addressed.

Social Needs

Gifted children frequently suffer from feelings of isolation. The child who thinks differently can feel alienated at any age. This can be especially painful during the teen years. Although one shouldn't be pushed into uncomfortable social situations, gifted children should be encouraged to maintain an open mind about making and keeping friends. Some gifted children who have been rejected from their peer group don't have a clue about how to solve their problems. Parents need to teach these children tactfulness and other social graces and help them learn the routines of everyday politeness.

One of the more common problems many gifted and talented children face today is perfectionism. These children drive themselves crazy trying to achieve their ideal of perfection. They do not accept perceived failure in themselves or others, and instead put an unhealthy amount of pressure upon themselves to succeed. Gifted and talented children need to be taught that learning in itself involves taking risks, and it doesn't always happen on the first try. They need to see people around them modeling nonperfectionist behaviors and acceptance of mistakes, their own as well as others.

Many times, problems arise because of the gap between the intellectual age and the emotional age of the child. Gifted children act silly and immature sometimes and parents want to tell them to "act their age." This is often exactly what they are doing. High intellectual ability does not always mean high emotional ability. Children benefit when parents and educators understand this and adjust expectations accordingly.

Many gifted children like the company of adults and older friends. They may feel the limitations of their own age group and interact better with adults rather than children their own age.

Another social need is that of the gifted child's perception. Gifted and talented children tend to be acutely aware of problems. It is common for them to develop fear and anger about global issues such as hunger, poverty, death, disease, etc. It is often helpful to set a good example and gradually expose them to the issues. Discussion about the feared "thing" is helpful to children who are determined to understand the concept.

Gifted children also have a tendency to be very sensitive. Their heightened awareness makes them vulnerable to feeling singled out. They feel that they are on the receiving end of many jokes. And they may feel overly guilty about their inability to control the situations around them. They tend to be acutely aware of their surroundings. All of these things combined can create a sensitivity overload. Gifted children may worry more about things and act more intensely than a typical child. Adults around them can help by modeling and talking openly with these children about their sensitivities and concerns. Enabling them to put their feelings in perspective leads to developing reasonable expectations.

Academic Needs

In addition to emotional and social concerns, gifted and talented children have obvious academic needs as well. Gifted children have an intense thirst for knowledge. They want to know a lot about many things or demonstrate a greater curiosity about a topic, often to the point of obsession. They display a consistent effort toward discovering more about their world. Many of their questions may be answered by parents, but many may need additional research. Parents can begin to gather reference materials such as books, videos, and computer programs. These will allow them more access to finding out about their interests.

Gifted children who demonstrate this drive to discover more about their world are often quite active, to the point of being mislabeled hyperactive. Gifted learners tend to have excellent memories and since their minds are often as active as their bodies, it is helpful for parents and educators to channel both energies. Gifted children also have a tendency to be very verbal, with an extensive vocabulary. This verbal "gift" can be encouraged in a number of ways in school so that it does not become a distraction to others.

Because they have an exceptional understanding of the world around them, gifted children tend to have a well-developed sense of humor. Parents and educators may want to monitor this humor so that it does not become sarcastic or cynical. Children need to see that those who put others down are never popular.

Almost all gifted children learn basic skills better and faster than children who are developmentally on target. They need less practice and repetition to learn new concepts. Gifted children benefit from having their academic curriculum extended or altered in some way to meet their specific needs. The regular school curriculum can be changed in various ways to meet the needs of gifted learners. Some schools group their children by ability, other districts have a separate

Chapter 15

CHOOSING TO ADOPT THE CHILD WITH SPECIAL NEEDS

THE STORY OF THE ORPHAN TRAIN RIDERS

Before the 1800s, if children lost their parents, they were usually raised by other family members or family friends. Legal adoptions were rare, though these children often went by the last name of the family raising them. The US government was not involved in these types of arrangements. The first American orphanage was established in 1729 in Natchez, Mississippi. It was run by Catholic nuns who cared for the children of settlers, many of whom were killed in Indian raids. There were only a handful of additional orphanages established over the next century. By the 1800s, though, there was a great increase of orphaned children and large orphanages sprang up in the East. Some of these orphanages housed up to 1000 children at a time.

It was during this period of our history that hundreds of thousands of people immigrated to the U.S. It was also during this time that our country began making the shift from being an agrarian society to one of urbanized economy. Up to 1870, one-half of the nation's adult workers were farmers. After this time, industry developed rapidly, greatly increasing the number of factories and demand for factory jobs. Also, more farm machinery meant less of a need for hired labor, displacing many farm workers. All of these events combined led to such a competition for factory jobs that wages were kept substantially low. People were not able to care for their families as before. Immigrants competed with displaced farm workers for factory jobs in the larger cities. There was no welfare system and so, in the case of families unable to find work, children of all ages were left to fend for themselves on the street. Parents often abandoned babies they felt unable to care for, or they sent older children, as young as six and seven, off when a new baby came into the family. Many young children worked entire days in factories, earning only a few pennies for their labor. Others found jobs shining shoes, peddling newspapers, selling matches, or other small jobs. Some were sent out to beg in the streets. Some ate from garbage cans or stole food to survive. It is estimated, that in 1850, when New York's population was 500,000, there were as many as 300,000 homeless children wandering the streets.

All children who lived in orphanages were called orphans, though many had parents who simply were unable to provide for them. In 1853, a minister named Charles Loring Brace started the Children's Aid Society to help these orphans. He was frustrated with the conditions of the large orphanages where children were not much better off than they had been on the street. Even in the orphanages, they were often abused and still went to bed hungry. He decided their greatest hope would be in finding new families. He also thought that he would find these families in the expansive west, which today we call the Midwest and South. He called this new program "placing out." Brace's vision and programs for orphaned children were the predecessor to today's foster care system.

Charles Brace and the Children's Aid Society soon began sending large numbers of orphaned children out west on what became known as orphan trains. Between 1854 and 1930, over 200,000 children rode the orphan trains.

Large groups of children were sent together on the trains. In preparation, they were given two new sets of clothes along with a coat, hat and shoes. Many were given a Bible. They were bathed, given haircuts and taught manners in the hope of making a positive impression on prospective adoptive parents.

The Children's Aid Society would send out flyers to cities and towns in the West and Midwest, advertising the future arrival of an orphan train. They would have the city choose a local committee who would approve the prospective adoptive families. However, the approval process was often haphazard at best. The committees generally approved anyone who showed interest in adopting without ascertaining why they wanted to adopt. Some families were simply looking for additional farmhands and treated the children as such. A few orphan train riders write of being poked and prodded, having dirty hands reach into their mouths to see how healthy their teeth were, just as one would look over a farm animal at auction.

Sometimes the trains would stop at several cities and have prospective adoptive parents choose their children from train stations along the route. More often, a destination city was chosen for the placing out. Upon arrival, the children would be cleaned up after the dusty ride. They would be fed and given a nap before the assigned meeting. The program would take place wherever there was a stage–a church, hotel, opera house, etc. The children would be lined upon the stage, standing or in chairs. Too often, siblings would be separated without the opportunity to say good-bye to each other. Orphan train agents, those who rode with the children, sometimes tried to keep brothers and sisters in the same general vicinity. In the early years of the orphan trains, Children's Aid Society workers tried to visit the children once a year to see how their placement was working. Soon, however, there were so many riders that it became more difficult to keep track of the placements. Also, many children went through several placements before finding a home. Some never found a permanent family.

Brace's orphan trains were considered an overall success and other organizations began trains as well. One was these was the Foundling Hospital in New York City. These were referred to as "baby trains" and the infants were placed with Catholic families throughout the West.

The orphan trains ran for over seventy-six years. In the first twenty years, an estimated 3,000 children were placed per year. The trains carried anywhere from a few, up to several hundred children on a trip that could last from a couple of days to a few weeks. Not every child who needed a home was able to ride an orphan train–those who were sick or considered disabled, those who had been in trouble with the authorities, children over the age of twelve (although there were a handful of children up to age seventeen who rode the trains), and children who were not of white European descent.

The trains were discontinued in the 1930s for several reasons. The Social Security Act was enacted by congress on August 14, 1935, as proposed by Franklin D. Roosevelt. It provided for federal grants to the states to help them meet the cost of programs for the aged, the blind, and dependent children. The federal grants also helped the states extend services for maternal and child care, children with disabilities and other child welfare services–leading to our modern day foster care system. From the 1930s, orphanages gave way to individual and small group foster homes. In addition, today, we are experiencing an increase in residential treatment facilities for children with special challenges.

FOSTER CARE TODAY

The present conundrum is the same today as it was during the orphan trains: a child's best interest versus biological family preservation. Children on the trains rarely were able to connect with their birth families as records were not kept, and Charles Loring Brace personally felt it best for the children to have a clean break. Over the years since, family preservation and reunification have had priority. Only recently has a new adoption initiative been launched which makes the best interest of the child a priority over birth family reunification. The new directive, as set forth by President Clinton on December 14, 1996, focuses on three main objectives:

1. Increasing the number of children who are adopted or permanently placed.

2. Moving children more rapidly from foster care to a permanent placement.

3. Raising adoption awareness in the public conscience.

President Clinton set the year 2002 as the goal for doubling–from 27,000 to 54,000–the number of foster children to find permanent placement each year. In order to reach this goal, the Department of Health and Human Services (DHHS) is working with states to set new target dates for permanent placements. The government is offering financial incentives to state agencies with increased placement rates. In addition, the administration is working toward improving placement rates by implementing and aggressively enforcing new laws that help to alleviate ethnic and racial barriers to permanent adoptive placement. These efforts follow the Multiethnic Placement Act of 1994 which calls for the "diligent recruitment of potential foster and adoptive families that reflect the ethnic and racial diversity of children...for whom foster and adoptive homes are needed." The Act also states that agencies receiving federal assistance may not "categorically deny to any person the opportunity to become an adoptive or foster parent, solely on the basis of the race, color, or national origin of the adoptive or foster parent, or the child, involved." In the final draft, the Act's intent is to "promote the best interests of children" by seeking foster and adoptive placements that "best meet each child's needs."

These are two of the strongest pieces of legislation regarding permanent placement to come out in recent years. However, for many, there are still questions as to the reality of their effectiveness, given the nature of the problems inherent in the foster care system. Consider the following: the government is parent to 502,000 children nationally, almost double the number in 1980; reports of child abuse and neglect have quadrupled nationally since the late 1970s (there were 969,000 confirmed abuse cases counted in 1996 by the National Committee to Prevent Child Abuse); federal aid in foster care programs has increased sixfold since the early 1980s making it our country's fastest growing entitlement program; a decade ago, when the crack phenomenon first arrived, New York's foster care system alone increased by a caseload of 10,000 children; 40 percent of children in foster care nationally are over the age eleven (making them extremely hard-to-place); 70 percent are over the age six; even with the new legislation, most older foster children are still more likely to finish out their childhood's in adolescent group homes, according to foster care officials in several large cities; the cost of having a child in the system for an average of seven years is well over $100,000, not counting psychotherapy and other counseling type services; recent studies in Sacramento, California and Hennepin County, Michigan reveal dramatic correlations between children growing up in the foster care system and the criminal justice system—these children, as adults, are found disproportionately in prisons, mental hospitals, and drug treatment programs; substance abuse is a factor in eight out of ten abuse and neglect cases nationally; and, now we are dealing with even newer drug phenomenons of methamphetamine and related drugs where there are not yet any comprehensive studies to determine the prenatal and long-term effects of these types of exposure on children.

There is yet another complication to consider when addressing the recent legislative changes—those parents who have adopted or fostered hard-to-place children learn that, too often, good intentions are simply not enough in adoption. Reiterating this is an example in Colorado that has made national headlines over the past couple of years. A two-year-old from a Russian orphanage was placed with a couple who had already adopted one child, a healthy infant, four years previously. The new young son was in their home for only eight months when paramedics rushed in to find him battered and brain dead. The mother stood trial and was convicted—she is currently serving a 40-year sentence. Her defense was what brought this case into the spotlight. Within weeks of the placement, the couple realized this child was drastically different from their first. They described the two-year-old as cold, manipulative, and violent. A therapist diagnosed severe reactive attachment disorder. This is an uncommon defense in a child abuse case. However, attachment disorders are one of the most severe behavioral problems of, not only postinstitutionalized children, but of those who have not received the nurture and love of a primary caregiver. Multiple foster care placements only exacerbate the problem.

Among others, symptoms can include destructiveness, lying, cruelty to other children and animals, fire-setting, and self-mutilation. The kinds of rage they experience is often extremely intense. Well-intentioned adoptive parents find themselves unable to continue parenting such children, and relinquish them back into the system or to other residential treatment facilities. These are the types of things that serve to compromise the strength of any legislative action—children, especially children with special challenges, don't easily conform to even the best intentions of caregivers.

OUR PERSONAL EXPERIENCES

Eleven years ago, we completed our first home-study. Since that time we have finalized six adoptions, had two birth children and have had a number of foster children. We went through the painful death of one son and we recently experienced one of the bleaker sides of adoption—a disrupted placement. We have always chosen to go through special needs programs, though the types of special challenges we have been opened to have changed over the years. Our last three placements have been with slightly older children instead of special needs infant programs. A couple of years ago, we became interested in a five-year-old from Texas. He had numerous medical and neurological challenges, but we felt much more confident with medical issues because of our previous adoptive experience. What we were not quite as prepared for were the attachment issues. Our dear friends had also taken on a five-year-old within a month of our placement. We often felt as if we were living parallel lives. Our sons had many of the same behaviors, which included a lack of emotion, aloofness, being manipulative, seeming to have an extremely high tolerance to pain (neither ever cried when falling off a bicycle or even when receiving updated immunizations), eating until they were physically sick, and never responding to or offering affection.

Like many adoptive families, we were initially excited about our new children. Both families had been through years of training and seminars on adopting older children. We both had other children. We felt prepared. The honeymoon stage for each of our families lasted less than a day, though it took many more months to fully realize the extent of the special challenges facing both new sons.

In our situation, we had concentrated on learning all we could about our child's medical and physical special needs before he was placed with us. We already had experience with seizure disorders; we learned Braille and researched cerebral palsy. These were the things his case-worker told us would be our greatest challenges. She never brought up the possibility of attachment issues, though any child who has been in the system for a number of years will probably have trust and bonding issues in varying degrees. And, the red flags were in his social history. However, like many adoptive parents, it is easy to dismiss those warnings before a placement–after all, most of us feel that the child just needs a new start in a loving home. What we don't always realize is that our "loving home" may not be enough to overcome the disturbance and maltreatment a child has experienced before placement.

We grew increasingly concerned over our son's lack of attachment to us, and, in turn, ours to him. We sought help from the school psychologist and social worker who both proved to be a tremendous support. With their encouragement, we began taking a second and closer look at our son's preplacement history. In addition to his medical needs, our child had been chronically neglected his first two years with his birth family. They had five other children and they were second generation in the government system. Our son had received very little nurture or stimulation as an infant. His first foster care placement lasted only a few months because the parents felt unable to care for all of his medical needs. His second was a lengthy placement where the foster parents did a tremendous job of getting him healthy and making him feel nurtured. However, when his foster father was in a serious accident, he was once again changing families and school situations. After the foster father began to mend, our son went back into their home. Because of the foster mother feeling overwhelmed after the accident and how it had changed their lives, she put the child into two different preschool situations: a bus picked him up early for morning preschool and another transferred him to an afternoon preschool, so again, he had numerous caretakers.

As our concerns for our son's behaviors and the feelings these behaviors brought out in us increased, we continued seeking therapeutic intervention. We were honest with our caseworker as she made her monthly visits and reports. She was very supportive and said the healthiest adoptive placements where attachment issues are predominant are the ones where parents are open enough to seek help. Oftentimes adoptive parents feel as if they have failed as parents when a placement moves beyond the honeymoon stage and the disruptive behaviors begin to dominate the family. As my friend once told me, "Even the most functional family can appear dysfunctional with a troubled child." Our son was with us for nine months and we were beginning to fill out the paperwork to finalize his adoption. We had just enrolled him in kindergarten and were looking forward to the new school year. His caseworker in Texas had her own concerns though. This was her very first case as a permanency worker. One of her comments to me once was, "I know this child inside and out, and the boy you are describing is not the child I know." Actually, she had only taken over his case six months before his placement with us and so I question her truly knowing the full extent of his challenges—his medical ones perhaps, but not his attachment issues. We continued to be forthright with our postplacement worker and the psychologist as to the problems we were facing, but we were continuing with the placement and our caseworker continued to recommend the placement be finalized. It took us completely by surprise then, when one afternoon, we found a message on our answering machine from our child's caseworker. She left a brief message saying she was terminating the placement and to have his things ready by the next morning. We were given less than 24 hours notice to transition him and the other children over this disruption. I found this kind of arbitrary power wielded by this caseworker frightening.

Most of our experiences with the social service system have been fairly positive and it is my guess that this was an unusual situation. I do find it ironic that birth parents who neglected this child, failed to follow through with his medication and immunizations, and who repeatedly missed visitation appointments were given several years to work on a reunification plan. On the other hand, we as his adoptive parents, repeatedly sought help for his special challenges, we tried to learn how to better love and bond to him, we caught him up on his immunizations and much needed dental work, and we never missed a postplacement visit. But, we were given only a day to say good-bye. I also feel strongly that this caseworker's actions will further add to this child's future attachment problems, when placement is attempted again. We recently learned the case worker is no longer employed as a permanency placement worker. Our relief over this chain of events is tempered by the fact that it has been almost a year since the disruption and this child remains in the foster care system with no immediate permanency placement plans.

I write of this experience not to dissuade prospective adoptive parents from choosing special needs adoption, but to underscore the absolute need for a personal support system. Over the years, we have found our support in our church family that has often provided meals, baby-sitting and transportation as we have gone through numerous hospitalizations of our children. We have found it through the IEP teams at our children's schools. We have actively sought it from those professionals in the mental health field. We have been given support by the many compassionate people who work for hospice. We have found it with other adoptive and foster parents, with family, friends, medical caregivers, and educational caregivers. And, in spite of our last experience, we have found it by being honest and open with our caseworkers about how a child's special challenges have, at times, changed our lives, our marriage, and the nature of our family. Special needs adoption is not a shortcut or a means for anxious, prospective adoptive parents to get a child faster. It is not easy, quick, or necessarily less expensive.

Good intentions are not always enough with specially challenged children, and love does not always overcome a horrendous past, especially those filled with abuse and neglect. My husband and I, along with many other parents, are still uncertain as to how much our love and good intentions will overcome the effects of prenatal drug and alcohol exposure.

However, I honestly find joy in the journey. I see the rewards with the heartbreak and I wouldn't change the route we have chosen. We have learned to change our perspective in our expectations—our children are different and face varying degrees of challenge. It is not easy, but I truly look forward to each new day with my children.

I hope the resources which follow offer additional support for those who are parents or caregivers of special needs children.

APPENDIX

RESOURCES FOR PRENATAL ALCOHOL AND DRUG EXPOSURE

National Organizations and Helplines:

National Organization on Fetal Alcohol Syndrome (NOFAS)
1815 H Street, NW Suite 750
Washington, DC 20006
800-666-6327

National Clearinghouse for Alcohol and Drug Information (NCADI)
P.O. Box 2345
Rockville, MD 20852
301-468-2600 & 800-729-6686

NAPARE (National Association for Perinatal Addiction Research and Education)
11 E. Hubbard Street, Suite 200
Chicago, IL 60611
NAPARE Alcohol, Drugs and Pregnancy Helpline:
1-800-638-2229

National Council on Alcoholism and Drug Dependence (NCADD)
12 West 21 Street
New York, NY 10010
212-206-6770
Helplines:
1-800-622-2255 or 1-800-475-4673

National Perinatal Information Center
One State Street, Suite 102
Providence, RI 02908
401-274-0650

Office for Substance Abuse Prevention (OSAP)
National Resource Center for the Prevention of Perinatal Abuse of Alcohol and

Other Drugs
9300 Lee Highway
Fairfax, VA 22031
703-218-5600

Children of Alcoholics Foundation
555 Madison Avenue
New York, NY 10022
212-754-0656

National Association for Children of Alcoholics
31586 South Coast Hwy., Suite 201
South Laguna, CA 92677
714-499-3899

National Association for Native American Children of Alcoholics
P.O. Box 18736
Seattle, WA 98118
206-222-5601

National Black Alcoholism Council
1629 K Street, NW, Suite 802
Washington, DC 20006
202-296-2696

National Coalition for Hispanic Health & Human Services
1501 16th Street, NW
Washington, DC 20036
202-387-5000

Alcoholics Anonymous (AA)
National Chapter
P.O. Box 9999
Van Nuys, CA 91409
818-780-3951

Al-Anon/Alateen Family Group Headquarters
P.O. Box 862, Midtown Station
New York, NY 10018
212-351-9500

Adult Children of Alcoholics
P.O. Box 862, Midtown Station
New York, NY 10018
800-344-2666

National Institute of Alcohol Abuse and Alcoholism
5600 Fishers Lane
Rockville, MD 20857

Cocaine Baby Helpline
800-327-BABE

Fetal Alcohol Education Program
Boston University School of Medicine
7 Kent Street
Brookline, MA 02146

Parents Helping Parents
535 Race Street, Suite 220
San Jose, CA 95126
408-288-5010

Adolescent Autonomy Project
Children's Rehab Center
2270 Ivy Road
Charlottesville, VA 22901
(804) 294-8184

Reading Resources:

Debbe Magnusen. *It's Never Dull.* The Cuddle Project, Inc. Also available at the same address: information about the Cuddle-Wrap swadding device for drug-addicted or preterm infants, 209 Technology Dr., Suite 200, Irvine, CA 92718.

Bolding, Kimm E. *Intricate Love: A First-Year Guide to Parenting Infants Affected by Substance Abuse.* Pikes Peak Foster Adopt Resources, Inc., P.O. Box 359, Colorado Springs, CO 80901.

Dorris, Michael. *The Broken Cord.* New York: Harper & Row, 1989.

Glinta, Carole T., & Ann P. Streissguth. Patients with Fetal Alcohol Syndrome and Their Caretakers. *Social Casework: The Journal of Contemporary Social Work:* 1988, pp. 453-459.

Groves, Pamela G. Effectively Dealing with Fetal Alcohol Syndrome. *The Counselor,* pp. 18-19, Nov./Dec., 1990.

Jones, K.I. and D.W. Smith. Recognition of the Fetal Alcohol Syndrome in Early Infancy. *Lancet,* 1:1973, pp. 999-1001.

Films

Honour of All. 1985. 56-minute videotape. Phil Lucas Production, Inc., P.O. box 1218, Issaquah WA 98027

One for My Baby. 1982. WHA Television Segment. 30 minutes, color. Friends of WHA Television, 821 Univ. Ave. Madison, WI 53706

Pregnancy on the Rocks: Fetal Alcohol Syndrome. 1982. 26 minutes, color. Peter Glaws Productions, 138 B. Avenue, Coronado, CA 92118.

RESOURCES FOR PRETERM AND NEWBORN COMPLICATIONS

National Organizations and Support Groups:

Parent Care, Inc.
101 1/2 S. Union St.
Alexandria, VA 22314-3323

Neonatal ICU Friends
E.W. Sparrow Hospital
1215 E. Michigan Ave.
Lansing, MI 48912
517-483-2700

National Perinatal Information Center
Providence, RI
401-274-0650

National Information Center for
Children and Youth with Disabilities (NICHCY)
P.O. Box 1492
Washington, DC 20013
703-893-6061 or 800-999-5599

International Council for Infant Survival
1515 Reistertown Rd. #300
Baltimore, MD 21208

National Sudden Infant Death Syndrome Foundation
310 S. Michigan Ave.
Chicago, IL 60604

Clothing and Diapers:

Preemie Pampers
Procter and Gamble CO., Inc.
800-543-4932

Preemie Pals (Cloth Diapers)
Nancy Nelson
1313 Harrington Ave. S.E.
Renton, WA 98058
206-271-0423

Cot'n tots
22 Lamont Ave.
San Antonio, TX 78209

For a Special Baby
1682 Roxanna St.
New Brighton, MN 55112

Shirey, Inc.
1017 Stanford Ave.
Greenville, TX 75401

I-C Manufacturing Co.
P.O. Box 1060
El Campo, TX 77518

S. Schwab Co., Inc.
P.O. Box 1417
Cumberland, MD 21502

Oh So Small
6432 Pacific Ave.
Tacoma, WA 98408

Paty, Inc.
4800 W. 34th St.
Houston, TX 77092

Premiers by Alexis
Warren Featherbone Co.
P.O. Box 393
Gainesville, GA 20501

Tiny Treasures for Molly and Friends
1060 23rd Ave. S.E.
Minneapolis, MN 55414

Very Important Preemie
312 Broad Ave.
Palisades Park, NJ 07650

Reading Resources:

Harrison, Helen. *The Premature Baby Book.* New York: St. Martin's Press, 1983.

Featherstone, Helen. *A Difference in the Family: Life with a Disabled Child.* New York: Basic Books, 1982.

Mulick, James A. & Seigfried M. Pueschel, eds. *Parent Professional Partnerships in Developmental Disability Services.* Cambridge, MA: Academic Guild Publishers, 1991

Tingey-Michailis, Carol. *Handicapped Infants and Children: A Handbook for Parents and Professionals.* Baltimore: University Park Press, 1983.

Weiner, Roberta & Jane Koppelman. *From Birth to 5: Serving the Youngest Handicapped Children.* Alexandria, VA: Capital Publications, 1987.

RESOURCES FOR DEVELOPMENTAL DISABILITIES

National Organizations and Support Groups:

Accent on Information
P.O. Box 700
Bloomington, IL 61702
309-378-2961

Alexander Graham Bell
Association for the Deaf, Inc.
3417 Volta Pl., NW
Washington, DC 20007
202-337-5220

Alliance of Genetic Support Groups
35 Wisconsin Cr. #440
Chevy Chase, MD 20815-7015
800-336-GENE
301-652-5553

American Academy for Cerebral Palsy and Developmental Medicine
1910 Byrd Ave., Suite 118
P.O. Box 11086
Richmond, VA 23230-1086
804-282-0036

American Academy of Pediatrics
141 Northwest Point Blvd.
P.O. Box 927
Elk Grove Village, IL 60009-0927
708-228-5005

American Academy of Ophthalmology
P.O. Box 7424
San Francisco, CA 94120-7242
415-561-8540

American Alliance for Health, Physical Education, Recreation and Dance
1900 Association Drive
Reston, VA 22091
703-476-3400

American Association for the Advancement of Science
Project on Science, Technology, and Disability
1333 H St., NW
Washington, DC 20005
202-326-6672

American Association on Mental Retardation (AAMR)
444 N. Capital St., NW, Suite 846
Washington, DC 20001
202-387-1968

American Association of University Affiliated Programs for Persons with Developmental Disabilities
8630 Fenton St., Suite 410
Silver Spring, MD 20910
301-588-8252

American Association on Mental Deficiency
1719 Kalorama Rd., NW
Washington, DC 20009

American Athletic Association for the Deaf
3701 Harrison Blvd., 2nd Floor
Ogden, UT 84403-2040
801-393-2263

American Bar Association
Child Advocacy Center
1800 M St., NW, Suite 200
Washington, DC 20036

American Civil Liberties Union
132 W. 43rd St.
New York, NY 10036

American Coalition of Citizens with Disabilities
1012 14th St., NW, Suite 901
Washington, DC 20036

American Council for the Blind
1010 Vermont Ave., NW, Suite 1100
Washington, DC 20005
202-393-3666
800-424-8666

American Deafness and Rehabilitation Association
P.O. Box 55369
Little Rock, AR 72225
501-868-8850

American Diabetes Association - National Center
1600 Duke St. P.O. Box 25757
Alexandria, VA 22314
703-549-1500

American Foundation for the Blind, Inc.
15 W. 16th St.
New York, NY 10011
212-620-2000
800-232-5463

American Heart Association
7320 Greenville Ave.
Dallas, TX 75231

American Occupational Therapy Association, Inc.
1383 Piccard Drive
Rockville, MD 20850
301-948-9626

American Optometric Association
243 North Lindberg
St. Louis, MO 63141
314-991-4100

American Physical Therapy Association (APTA)
1111 N. Fairfax St.
Alexandria, VA 22314
800-999-2728

American Printing House for the Blind (APHB)
P.O. Box 6085
Louisville, KY 40206-0085
502-895-2405

American Self-Help Clearinghouse
St. Clares-Riverside Medical Center
25 Pocono Rd.
Denville, NJ 07834-2995
201-625-7101 or 201-625-9053 (TDD)

American Society for Deaf Children (ASDC)
2848 Arden Way
Sacramento, CA 95825-1373
800-942-ASDC or 916-482-0120 (TDD)

American Speech-Language-Hearing Association (ASHA)
1801 Rockville Pike
Rockville, MD 20852
301-897-5700

The ARC (Association for Retarded Citizens)
500 E. Border St., Suite 300
Arlington, TX 76010
817-261-6003

ASA International Affairs Committee
Autism Training Center
Old Main 316 - Marshall University
Huntington, WV 25701
304-696-2332

Associated Services for the Blind
919 Walnut St.
Philadelphia, PA 19107
215-627-3501

Association of Birth Defect Children
827 Irma St.
Orlando, FL 32803
800-313-ABDC or 407-245-7035

Association for the Care of Children's Health (ACCH)
1910 Woodmont Ave., Suite 300
Bethesda, MD 20814
301-654-6549

Association for Children with Down Syndrome
2616 Martin Ave.
Bellmore, NY 11710
516-221-4700

Association for Persons with Severe Handicaps (TASH)
29 W. Susquehanna Ave., Suite 210
Baltimore, MD 21204
410-828-8274

Association for Education and Rehabilitation of the Blind and Visually Impaired
206 N. Washington St.
Alexandria, VA 22314
703-548-1884

Association on Higher Education and Disability (AHEAD)
P.O. Box 21192
Columbus, OH 43221
614-488-4972

Association of Neurometabolic Disorders
5223 Brookfield Lane
Sylvania, OH 43560-1809
419-885-1497

Autism Network International
P.O. Box 448
Syracuse, NY 13210-0448

Autism Research Institute
4182 Adams Ave.
San Diego, CA 92116

Autism Society of America
8601 Georgia Ave., Suite 503
Silver Spring, MD 20910
301-565-0433

Avenues
P.O. Box 5192
Sonora, CA 95370
209-928-3688

Blind Children's Fund
1975 Rutgers Circle
East Lansing, MI 48823
517-332-2666

Boy Scouts of America
1325 Walnut Hill La.
Irving, TX 75062
214-580-200

Candlelighters Childhood Center Foundation
7910 Woodmont Ave., Suite 460
Bethesda, MD 20814
800-366-2223 (TTY) or 301-657-8401

Captioned Films/Videos
5000 Park St. N.
St. Petersburg, FL 33709
800-237-6213 (Voice/TTY) or 813-541-7571

Center on Human Development
Division of Special Education and Rehabilitation
Clinical Services Bldg. - College of Education
Eugene, OR 97403-1211

Centers for Disease Control National AIDS/HIV Hotline
800-342-AIDS (2437)
800-344-SIDA (7432) Spanish Access
800-AIDS-TTY (1-800-243-7889)

Centers for Disease Control National AIDS Information Clearinghouse
P.O. Box 6003
Rockville, MD 20849-6003
800-458-5231 or 800-243-7012(TTY/TDD)

Child and Adolescent Services System Program (CASSP)
National Institute of Mental Health
Georgetown University Child Development Center
3800 Resvoir Rd., NW
Washington, DC 20007

Children and Adults with Attention Deficit Disorders (CH.A.D.D.)
49 NW 70th Ave., Suite 109
Plantation, FL 33317
305-587-3700

Children's Brain Diseases Foundation
350 Parnassus Ave., Suite 900
San Francisco, CA 94117
415-565-6259

Children's Defense Fund
25 E St., NW
Washington, DC 20001
202-628-8787

Christian Council of Persons with Disabilities
7120 West Dove Ct.
Milwaukee, WI 53223
414-357-6672

Clearinghouse on Disability Information
Office of Special Education and Rehabilitative Services (ORERS)
U.S. Dept. of Education
Room 3132, Switzer Bldg.
Washington, DC 20202-2524
202-708-5366

Cleft Palate Foundation
1218 Grandview Ave.
Pittsburg, PA 15211
412-481-1376 or 1-800-24-CLEFT

Coalition on Sexuality and Disability, Inc.
122 East 23rd St.
New York, NY 10010
212-242-3900

Commission on the Mentally Disabled
American Bar Association
1800 M St., NW
Washington, DC 20036

Compassionate Friends
P.O. Box 3696
Oak Brook, IL 60522-3696
708-990-0010

Corneal Dystrophy Foundation
1926 Hidden Creek Drive
Kingwood, TX 77339
713-358-4227

Cornelia de Lange Syndrome Foundation, Inc.
60 Dyer Ave.
Collinsville, CT 06022
203-693-0159

Council for Exceptional Children (CEC)
1920 Association Drive
Reston, VA 22091-1589
703-620-3660

Council of Families with Visual Impairment
c/o American Council of the Blind
1155 15th Street, NW, Suite 720
Washington, DC 20005
202-393-3666

Council on Family Health
225 Park Ave., South, 17th Floor
New York, NY 10003
212-598-3617

Cystic fibrosis Foundation
6931 Arlington Rd.
Bethesda, MD 20814
800-FIGHT CF (344-4823) or 301-951-4422

DB-Link: The National Information Clearinghouse on Children Who Are Deaf-Blind
c/o Teaching Research
Northwestern Oregon State College
345 North Monmouth Ave.
Monmouth, OR 97361
503-838-8756

Deafness Research Foundation
9 E. 38th St.
New York, NY 10016
212-684-6556
212-684-6559(TTY)

Deafpride
1350 Potomac Ave., SE
Washington, DC 20003
202-675-6700 (Voice/TTY)

Direct Link for the disABLED, Inc.
P.O. Box 1036
Solvang, CA 93464
805-688-1603 (Voice/TDD)

Disabilities Rights Education and Defense Fund (DREDF)
2212 Sixth St.
Berkeley, CA 94710
510-644-2555 (Voice/TDD)

Dyslexia Research Institute, Inc.
4745 Centerville Rd.
Tallahassee, FL 32308
904-893-2216

Early Recognition Intervention Network (ERIN)
P.O. Box 637
Carlisle, MA 01741
508-287-0920

Epilepsey Foundation of America
4351 Garden City Drive
Landover, MD 20785-2267
800-EFA-1000 or 800-332-2070 (TDD)

ERIC Clearinghouse on Disabilities and Gifted Education
1920 Association Drive
Reston, VA 22091-1589
800-328-0272 or 703-620-3660 (TDD)

Exceptional Parent
209 Harvard St., Suite 303
Brookline, MA 02146
617-730-5800 or 617-730-9856 (TDD)

Families of Children Under Stress (FOCUS)
3813 Briargreen Ct.
Doraville, GA 30340
404-934-7529

FEDCAP Rehabilitation Services, Inc.
211 W. 14th St.
New York, NY 10011
212-727-4200 or 212-727-4384 (TDD)

Federation for Children With Special Needs
95 Berkeley St., Suite 104
Boston, MA 02116
800-331-0688 or 617-482-2915 (Voice/TTY)

Federation of Families for Children's Mental Health
1021 Prince St.
Alexandria, VA 22314-2971
703-684-7710

Fighters for Encephaly Defects Support (FEDS)
3032 Brereton St.
Pittsburg, PA 15219
412-687-6437

Financing Health Care for Chronically Ill and Disabled Children
Albert Einstein College of Medicine–Dept. of Pediatrics
1410 Pelham Pkwy., South
New York, NY 10461
212-822-3895

Foundation for Glaucoma Research
490 Post St., suite 830
San Francisco, CA 94102
415-986-3162

Fragile X Foundation
P.O. Box 300233
Denver CO 80203

Gesell Institute of Human Development
310 Prospect St.
New Haven, CT 06511
203-777-3481

Girl Scouts of the U.S.A.
830 Third Ave.
New York, NY 10022
212-940-7500

Hadley School for the Blind
700 Elm St.
Winnetka, IL 60093
708-446-8111 or 800-323-4238

Hearing Aid Helpline
20361 Middlebelt Rd.
Livonia, MI 48152
800-521-5247

Helen Keller International
90 Washington St., 15th Floor
New York, NY 10006
212-943-0890

Helen Keller National Center for Deaf-Blind Youths and Adults
111 Middle Neck Rd.
Sands Point, NY 11050
516-944-8900

Hereditary Disease Foundation
1427 7th St., Suite 2
Santa Monica, CA 90401
310-458-4183

Hilton/Perkins National and International Program
Perkins School for the Blind
175 North Beacon St.
Watertown, MA 02172
617-924-3434

Howard University Center for Sickle Cell Disease
2121 Georgia Ave., NW
Washington, DC 20059
202-806-7930

Hydrocephalus Association
870 Market St., Suite 955
San Francisco, CA 94102
415-776-4713

Hydrocephalus Support Group
P.O. Box 4236
Chesterfield, MO 63006
314-532-8228

IBM National Support Center of Persons with Disabilities
P.O. Box 2150
Atlanta, GA 30055
800-IBM-2133

Independent Living Aids, Inc.
27 E. Mall
Plainview, NY 11803
516-752-8080

In Door Sports Club, Inc.
1145 Highland St.
Napoleon, OH 43545
419-592-5756

IN*SOURCE, Indiana Resource Center for Families with Special Needs
833 Northside Blvd., Bldg. #1-Rear
South Bend, IN 46617
219-234-7101

Institute for Child Behavior Research
4182 Adams Ave.
San Diego, CA 92116

International Institute for Visually Impaired
230 Central Street
Auburndale, MA 02166
617-332-2133

International Organization for the Education of the Hearing Impaired
3417 Volta Place, NW
Washington, DC 20007
202-337-5220 (Voice/TDD)

International Rett Syndrome Association
9121 Piscataway Rd., Suite 2B
Clinton, MD 20735
301-856-3334

International Shriners Headquarters
2900 Rocky Point Drive
Tampa, FL 33607
800-237-5055 or 813-281-0300

Job Accomodation Network (JAN)
West Virginia University
918 Chestnut Ridge Rd., Suite 1
P.O. Box 6080
Morgantown, WV 26506-6080
800-526-7234

John Tracy Clinic (Correspondence courses on deaf-blindness sign language)
806 W Adams Blvd.
Los Angeles, CA 90007
213-748-5481

Joseph P. Kennedy, Jr., Foundation
1350 New York Ave., NW, Suite 500
Washington, DC 20005-4709
202-393-1250

Judge David L. Bazelon Mental Health Law Center
1101 15th St., NW, Suite 1212
Washington, DC 20005
202-467-5730 or 202-467-4232 (TTY)

Kesher-Jewish Parents of Children with Special Needs
3525 W Peterson, Suite T-17
Chicago, IL 60659
312-588-0551

Kids on the Block (puppet show available in 49 states)
9385 C Gerwig Lane
Columbia, MD 21046
800-368-KIDS

La Leche League International, Inc.
9616 Minneapolis Ave.
Franklin Park, IL 60131
312-455-7730

Learning Disabilities Association of America
4156 Library Rd.
Pittsburg, PA 14234
412-341-1515 or 412-341-8077

Lethbridge Society for Rare Disorders
#2-740-4 Ave. South
Lethbridge, Alberta, 0N4 T1J
CANADA
403-329-0665

Lions Club International (Issues related to visual impairments)
300 22nd Street
Oak Brook, IL 60521-8842
708-571-5466

Library of Congress
National Library Service for the Blind and Physically Disabled
1291 Taylor St., NW
Washington, DC 20542
800-424-8567

MAINSTREAM
1200 15th St. NW
Washington, DC 20005
202-833-1136

March of Dimes Birth Defect Foundation
1275 Mamaroneck Ave.
White Plains, NY 10605
914-428-7100

Mobility International
P.O. Box 10767
Eugene, OR 97440
503-343-1284 (Voice/TDD)

Mothers United for Moral Support, Inc. (MUMS)
150 Cluster St.
Green Bay, WI 54301
414-336-5333

Muscular Dystrophy Association
3561 E. Sunrise Dr.
Tuscon, AZ 85718-3208
602-529-2000

National Association of Developmental Disabilities Councils
1234 Massachusetts Ave., NW, Suite 103
Washington, DC 20005
202-347-1234

National Association for Parents of the Visually Impaired
P.O. Box 317
Watertown, MA 02272-0317
800-562-6265

National Association for Perinatal Addiction Research and Education (NAPARE)
200 N. Michigan
Chicago, IL 60601
312-541-1272

National Association of Private Schools for Exceptional Children
1522 K St., NW, Suite 1032
Washington, DC 20005
202-408-3338

National Association of Protection and Advocacy Systems
900 Second St., NE, Suite 221
Washington, DC 20005
202-408-9514 or 202-408-9521 (TDD)

National Association of State Directors of Developmental Disabilities Service
113 Oronco St.
Alexandria, VA 22314
703-683-4202

National Association for Visually Handicapped
22 West 21st St., 6th Floor
New York, NY 10010
212-889-3141

National Association of Work Force Developmental Professionals
1620 I St., NW
Washington, DC 20006
202-887-6120

National Attention Deficit Disorder Association (NADDA)
19262 Jamboree Rd.
Irvine, CA 92715
For membership in NADDA, write:
P.O. Box 488
West Newbury, MA 01985
800-487-2282

National Autism Hotline/Autism Services Center
605 Ninth St.
Prichard Bldg.
P.O. Box 507
Huntington, WV 25710-0507
304-525-8014

National Birth Defects Center
40 Second Ave.
Waltham, MA 02154
617-466-9555

National Braille Association, Inc.
3 Towline Circle
Rochester, NY 14623-2513
716-473-0900

National Braille Press
88 St. Stephen Street
Boston, MA 02116
617-266-6160

National Camps for Blind Children
4444 South 52nd Street
Lincoln, NE 68516
402-488-0981

National Captioning Institute (NCI), Inc.
1900 Gallows Rd.
Vienna, VA 22182
800-533-9673 or 800-321-8337 (TDD)

National Catholic Office for Persons With Disabilities
P.O. Box 29113
Washington, DC 20017
202-529-2933 (Voice/TDD)

National Center for Education in Maternal and Child Health
38th and R Sts., NW
Washington, DC 20057
202-625-8400

National Center for Law and the Deaf
Gallaudet University
800 Florida Ave., NE
Washington, DC 20002-3695
202-651-5373 (Voice/TDD)

National Center for Learning Disabilities (NCLD)
381 Park Ave., S, Suite 1420
New York, NY 10016
212-545-7510 or 212-687-7211

National Center for Stuttering, Inc.
200 E. 33rd St.
New York, NY 10016
800-221-2483

National Center for Youth With Disabilities
University of Minnesota, box 721
420 Delaware St., SE
Minneapolis, MN 55455-0392
612-626-2825 or 612-624-3939 (TDD)

National Clearinghouse on Post-secondary Education for Individuals with Disabilities
HEATH (Higher Education and Adult Training for People with Disabilities)
Resource Center
One Dupont Circle, Suite 800
Washington, DC 20036-1193
800-333-6293 or 800-54H-EATH or 202-939-9320

National Committee for Citizens in Education
900 Second St. NE, Suite 8
Washington, DC 20002
202-544-9495

National Council on Independent Living
2111 Wilson Blvd., Suite 405
Arlington, VA 22201
703-525-3406 or 518-274-1979

National Down Syndrome Congress (NDSC)
1605 Chantilly Drive, Suite 250
Atlanta, GA 30324
800-232-6372 or 404-633-1555

National Down Syndrome Society
666 Broadway, Suite 810
New York, NY 10012
800-221-4602 or 212-460-9330

National Easter Seal Society
230 West Monroe St., Suite 1800
Chicago, IL 60606
800-221-6827 or 312-726-6200 or 312-726-4258 (TDD)

The National Epilepsy Library and Resource Center
4351 Garden City Drive
Landover, MD 20785
301-459-3700

National Federation of the Blind
1800 Johnson St.
Baltimore, MD 21230
410-659-9314

National Foundation of Denistry for the Handicapped
1800 Glen Arm Place, Suite 500
Denver, CO 80202
303-298-9650

National Foundation for Jewish Genetic Diseases
250 Park Ave., Suite 1000
New York, NY 10177
212-371-6155

National Fragile X Foundation
1441 York St., Suite 2156
Denver, CO 80206
800-688-8765 or 303-333-6155

National Handicapped Sports
National Headquarters
451 Hungerford Dr., Suite 100
Rockville, MD 20850
301-393-7505 or 301-217-0963 (TDD)

National Head Injury Foundation (NHIF)
1776 Massachusetts Ave., NW, Suite 100
Washington, DC 20036-1904
800-444-6443 (Helpline) or 202-296-6443

National Hydrocephalus Foundation
400 N Michigan Ave., Suite 1102
Chicago, IL 60611-4102
815-467-6548

National Information Center for Children and Youth with Disabilities (NICHCY)
P.O. Box 1492
Washington, DC 20013
800-695-0285 (Voice/TDD)

National Information Center on Deafness
Gallaudet University
800 Florida Ave. NE
Washington, DC 20002-3695
202-651-5051 or 202-651-5052 (TDD)

National Information Center for Educational Media (NICEM)
P.O. Box 40130
Albuquerque, NM 87196
800-468-3453 or 505-265-3591

National Information System Clearinghouse Center for Developmental Disabilities
University of South Carolina, Benson Bldg.
Columbia, SC 29208
800-922-9234

National Institute of Neurological Disorders and Stroke
9000 Rockville Pike, Bldg. 31
Room 8A-16
Bethesda, MD 20892
301-496-5751

National Lekotec Center (toy lending services for children with special needs)
2100 Ridge Ave.
Evanston, IL 60204

National Library Service for the Blind and Physically Disabled
Library of Congress
1291 Taylor St., NW
Washington, DC 20542
202-70705100 or 202-707-0744

National Mental Health Association
1021 Prince St.
Alexandria, VA 22314-2971
800-969-6642 or 703-684-7722

National Network to Prevent Birth Defects
Box 15309 SE Station
Washington, DC 20003
202-543-5450

National Neurofibromatosis Foundation
141 Fifth Ave., Suite 7-S
New York, NY 10010-7105
800-323-7938 or 212-460-8980 (Voice/TDD)

National Organization of Parents of Blind Children
1800 Johnson St.
Baltimore, MD 21230
410-659-9314

National Organization on Disability
910 16th St., Suite 600
Washington, DC 20006
800-248-ABLE or 202-293-5960 or 301-293-5968 (TDD)

National Organization for Albinism and Hypopigmentation (NOAH)
1500 Locust St., Suite 1816
Philadelphia, PA 19102
215-545-2322 or 800-473-2310

National Organization for Rare Disorders (NORD)
100 Route 37, P.O. Box 8923
New Fairfield, CT 06812-8923
800-999-NORD or 203-746-6518 or 203-746-6972 (TDD)

National Parent Network on Disabilities (NPND)
1600 Prince St., Suite 115
Alexandria, VA 22314
703-684-NPND or 703-684-6763 (Voice/TDD)

National Rehabilitation Clearinghouse
816 W 6th St.
Oklahoma State University
Stillwater, OK 74078
405-624-7650

National Rehabilitation Information Center
8455 Colesville Rd.
Silver Spring, MD 20910
800-346-2742 (Nat. Rehab.) 800-227-0216 (Voice/TDD)

National Scoliosos Foundation, Inc.
72 Mt. Auburn St.
Watertown, MA 02172
617-926-0397

National Self-Help Clearinghouse
Graduate School/University Center
CUNY
25 West 43rd St., Room 620
New York, NY 10036
212-642-2944

National Society to Prevent Blindness
500 E. Remington Rd.
Schaumburg, IL 60173
800-221-3004 or 708-843-2020

National Spinal Cord Injury Association
545 Concord Ave., Suite 29
Cambridge, MA 02138
800-962-9629 (Hotline) or 617-935-2722

National Spinal Cord Injury Hotline
Montbello Hospital
2201 Argonne Drive
Baltimore, MD 21218
800-526-3456 or 410-366-2325

National Tay-Sachs and Allied Disease Association
2001 Beacon St., Suite 204
Brookline, MA 02146
617-277-4463

National Tuberous Sclerosis Association
8000 Corporate Drive, Suite 120
Landover, MD 20785
800-225-NTSA or 301-459-9888

National Wheelchair Athletic Association
3595 E Fountain Blvd., Suite 382
Colorado Springs, CO 80910
719-574-1150

The Newington, Connecticut ABELDATA Resource Center
(Toy and specialized equipment)
800-344-5405

Neuro-Development Treatment Association (NDTA)
P.O. Box 14613
Orton Dyslexia Society
8600 LaSalle Rd.
Chester Bldg., Suite 382
Baltimore, MD 21286-2044
800-ABCD-123 (800-222-3123) or 410-296-0232

PACER Center, Inc. (Parent Advocacy Coalition for Educational Rights)
4826 chicago Ave., South
Minneapolis, MN 55417-1055
612-827-2966 (Voice/TDD)

PAM Assistance Centre
601 Maple St.
Lansing, MI 48906-5038
800-274-7426 or 517-371-5897

Parent Information Center
155 Manchester St.
P.O. Box 1422
Concord, NH 03301
603-224-6299

Parents Educating Parents
Georgia/ARC
1851 Ram Runway, Suite 104
College Park, GA 30337
404-761-2745

Parents Advocating Vocational Education (PAVE)
6316 S 12th St.
Tacoma, WA 98645
206-565-2266

Parents of Chronically Ill Children
1527 Maryland St.
Springfield, IL 62702
217-522-6810 (Voice/TDD)

Parent Educational Advocacy Training Center
10340 Democracy Lane
Fairfax, VA 22030
703-691-7826 (Voice/TTY)

Parentele: An Alliance of Parents and Friends Networking for Those with
Special Needs
310 S. Jersey St.
Denver, CO 80224

The Parent/Professional Partnership Resource Exchange
2150 Brisbane Ave.
Reno, NV 89503
702-747-7751

President's Committee on Employment of People with Disabilities
1331 F St., NW
Washington, DC 20004-1107
202-376-6200 or 202-376-6205 (TDD)

President's Committee on Mental Retardation (PCMR)
330 Independence Ave.
Cohen Bldg., Room 5325
Washington, DC 20201
202-619-0634 or 202-205-9519

Project STAR
1800 Columbus Ave.
Roxbury, MA 02119
617-442-7442

Recording for the Blind and Dyslexic (RFB&D)
20 Rozel Rd.
Princeton, NJ 08540
800-221-4792

Rehabilitation Research and Training Center
Virginia Commonwealth University
1314 W Main St.
Richmond, VA 23284-0001

Research and Training Center for Accessible Housing
North Carolina State University School of Design
Box 8613
Raleigh, NC 27695-8613
919-515-3082

RP Foundation Fighting Blindness
(National Retinitis Pigmentosa Foundation, Inc.)
Executive Plaza 1, Suite 800
11350 McCormick Rd.
Hunt Valley, MD 21031-1014
410-785-1414 or 800-683-5555

Scoliosis Research Society
6300 N River Rd., Suite 727
Rosemont, IL 60018-4226
708-698-1627

Self Help for Hard of Hearing People (SHHH)
7910 Woodmont Ave., Suite 1200
Bethesda, MD 20814
301-657-2248 or 301-657-2249 (TDD)

Senate Document Room
Hart Bldg
Washington, DC 20515
202-225-7860

House Document Room
Room B-18
House Annex #2
Washington, DC 20515
202-225-3456
Both of these can provide copies of federal bills or laws.

Siblings Information Network
The A.J. Pappanikou Center on Special Rehabilitation
62 Washington St.
Middletown, CT 06457-2844
203-344-7500 or 203-344-7590 (TDD)

Siblings for Significant Change
United Charities Bldg.
105 E 22nd St., Room 710
New York, NY 10010
212-420-0766

Sickle Cell Disease Association of America, Inc.
3345 Wilshire Blvd., Suite 1106
Los Angeles, CA 90010
800-421-8453 or 213-736-5455

Signing Exact English (SEE) Center for the Advancement of Deaf Children
P.O. Box 1181
Los Alamitos, CA 90720
310-430-1467 (Voice/TTY)

Social Security Administration (SSA)
1350 New York Ave., NW, Suite 500
Washington, DC 20005-4709
202-523-0412

Special Education Software Center
800-426-2133

Specialnet
GTE Education Services, Inc
2021 K Street, NW
Washington, DC 20006
202-835-7300

Special Olympics International
1350 New York Ave., NW, Suite 500
Washington, DC 20005-4709
202-628-3630

Special Recreation, Inc.
362 Koser Ave.
Iowa City, IA 52246-3038
319-7578 or 319-353-6808

Spina Bifida Association of America
4590 MacArthur Blvd., NW, #250
Washington, DC 20007-4226
800-621-3141 or 202-944-3285

TEACCH (Treatment and Education of Autistic and Related Communication
Handicapped Children and Adults)
Division TEACCH, CB#7180
Medical School Wing E
Chapel Hill, NC 27599-7180
919-966-2174

Team of Advocates for Special Kids (TASK)
100 W. Cerritos Ave.
Anaheim, CA 92805
714-533-TASK

Technical Assistance for Parent Programs (TAPP)
312 Stuart St., 2nd Floor
Boston, MA 02116
617-482-2915

Technical Assistance for Special Populations Program (TASPP)
National Center for Research in Vocational Education
University of Illinois Site
345 Education Bldg.
1310 S Sixth St.
Champaign, IL 61820
217-333-0807

THRESHOLD-Intractable Seizure Disorder Support Group
26 Stavola Rd.
Middletown, NJ 07748-3728
908-957-0714

Tourette Syndrome Association
42-40 Bell Blvd.
Bayside, NY 11361
212-224-2999

Trace Center and Development Center
1500 Highland Ave., S-151
Madison, WI 53705-2280
608-262-6966 or 608-263-5408 (TDD)

United Cerebral Palsy Association, Inc.
1522 K St., NW #1112
Washington, DC 20005-1202
800-872-5827 or 202-842-1266 (Voice/TTY)

U.S. Architectural Transportation Barriers Compliance Board
1331 F St., NW, Suite 1000
Washington, DC 20004-1111
800-USA-ABLE or 202-272-5449 (TDD)

United States Association for Blind Athletes
33 North Institute St.
Colorado Springs, CO 80903
719-630-0422

World Rehabilitation Fund
386 Park Ave. S, Suite 500
New York, NY 10016-4901

EDUCATIONAL RESOURCES

National Organizations and Support Groups:

ADDA (Attention-Deficit Disorder Association)
4300 West Park Blvd.
Plano, TX 75093

ADDAG (Attention Deficit Disorder Advocacy Group)
8091 South Ireland Way
Aurora, CO 80016
303-690-7548

ADDendum
Box 296
Scarborough, NY 10510

AFT Teachers' Network for Education or the Handicapped
555 New Jersey Avenue, NW
Washington, DC 20001
202-879-4460

Association for Children and Adults with Learning Disabilities
National Headquarters
4156 Library Road
Pittsburg, PA 15234
412-341-1516

Attention Please! (Bimonthly newsletter for children with ADD)
2106 Third Avenue North
Seattle, WA 98109-2304

Center for Law and Education
Larsen Hall, 6th Floor
14 Appian Way
Cambridge, MA 02138
617-495-4666

Foundation for Science and the Handicapped, Inc. (FISH)
154 Juliet Court
Clarendon Hills, IL 60514
312-323-1481

Independent Living Research Utilization Project (ILRU)
The Institute for Rehabilitation and Research
P.O. Box 20095
Houston, TX 77225
National resource center for independent living

Learning Disabilities Association of America
4156 Library Rd.
Pittsburg, PA 14234
412-341-1515 or 412-341-8077

Mexican-American Legal Defense & Education Fund
604 Mission St., 10th Floor
San Francisco, CA 94105
415-543-5598

National Association of the Deaf Legal Defense Fund
P.O. Box 2304
800 Florida Ave., NE
Washington, DC 20002
202-466-6896

National Center for Learning Disabilities (NCLD)
381 Park Ave., S, Suite 1420
New York, NY 10016
212-545-7510 or 212-687-7211

National Committee of Citizens in Education
10840 Little Patuxent Pkwy., Suite 301
Columbia, MD 21044
301-997-9300 or 800-NETWORK

National Juvenile Law Center
St. Louis University School of Law
3701 Lindell Blvd.
St. Louis, MO 63108
314-652-5555

Registry of Interpreters for the Deaf, Inc. (RID)
814 Thayer Ave
Silver Spring, MD 20910
301-588-2406

STOMP (Specialized Training of Military Parents)
  The STOMP Project assists military families residing in the U.S. or stationed overseas.

West Coast Office:
STOMP
12208 Pacific Highway, SW
Tacoma, WA 98499
206-588-1741

East Coast Office:
STOMP
ARC/Georgia STOMP Project
1851 Ram Runway, #104
College Park, GA 30337
404-568-0042

United Together (UT)
348 Haworth Hall
Lawrence, KS 66045
913-864-4950

Federal Offices

Department of Education:

Administration on Developmental Disabilities
Office of Developmental Services
330 C Street, SW, Room 3070
Washington, DC 20201
202-245-2890

Bureau of Indian Affairs
1951 Constitution Ave., NW
Washington, DC 20202
202-343-5831

National Council on Disability
800 Independence Ave., SW
Washington, DC 20591
202-267-3846

National Institute of Education
Brown Bldg.
19th and M Streets, NW
Washington, DC, 20208
202-254-5740

Office of Special Education and Rehabilitative Services
330 C Street, SW
Mary Switzer Bldg
Washington, DC 20202
202-732-1245

Office of Special Education Programs
330 C Street, SW
Mary Switzer Bldg.
Washington, DC 20202
202-732-1282

Rehabilitative Services Administration
330 C Street, SW, Room 3028
Mary Switzer Bldg.
Washington, DC 20202
202-732-1282

Office for Civil Rights
303 Independence Avenue, SW
Washington, DC 20201
202-245-6118

READING RESOURCES

DEVELOPMENTAL DISABILITY, EDUCATION AND CHILDHOOD MENTAL DISABILITY

Developmental Disability:

Adams, Ronald C., Alfred H. Daniel, & Lee Rullman. *Games, Sports, and Exercises for the Physically Handicapped*, 3d ed. Philadelphia: Lea and Febiger, 1982.

American Foundation for the Blind. *Directory of Services for Blind and Visually Impaired Persons in the United States and Canada*, 24th ed. New York: Author, 1993.

Appolloni, Tony, & Thomas P. Cooke. *A New Look at Guardianship: Protective Services That Support Personalized Living.* Baltimore: Paul H. Brookes, 1984.

Association for the Care of Children's Health. *Organizing and Maintaining Support Groups for Parents of Children with Chronic Ilness and Handicapping Conditions.* Washington, DC: ACCH, 1986.

Atack, Sally M. *Art Activities for the Handicapped.* Englewood Cliffs, NJ: Prentice-Hall, 1982.

Ayres, A. Jean. *Sensory Integration and the Child.* Los Angeles: Western Psychological Services, 1979.

Baker, B., Brightman, & A, Blacher, J., Heifetz, Louis, Hinshaw, S., and Murphy, D. *Steps to Independence: A Skills Trainong Guide for Parents and Teachers of Children with Special Needs.* 2nd ed. Baltimore: Paul H. Brookes, 1989.

Barkley, R.A. *Attention-Deficit hyperactivity disorder—A handbook for diagnosis and treatment.* New York: Guilford Press, 1990.

Batshaw, M.L. *Your Child has a disability. A complete sourcebook of daily and medical care.* Boston: Little, Brown, 1991.

Becker, W.C. *Parents Are teachers: A child managment program.* Champaign, IL: Research Press, 1971

Bergman, T. *Seeing in Special Ways: Children Living with Blindness.* Milwaukee, WI: Gareth Stevens, 1988.

Bloom, B. & Seljeskog, E. *A Parent's Guide to Spina Bifida.* Minneapolis: University of Minnesota Press, 1988.

Bolton, S. *One Step at a Time: A Manual for Families of Children with Hearing and Vision Impairments.* Monmouth, OR: Teaching Research, 1990.

Brennan, M. *Show Me How: A Manual for Parents of Preschool Visually Impaired and Blind Children.* New York: American Foundation for the Blind, 1982.

Bruinicks, R.H., & K.C. Lakin. *Living and Learning in the Least Restrictive Environment.* Baltimore: Paul H. Brookes, 1985.

Buist, Charlotte A. & Jerome L. Schulman. *Toys and Games for Educationally Handicapped Children.* Springfield, IL: Charles C Thomas, 1976.

Buscaglila, Leo. *The Disabled and Their Parents: A Counseling Challenge.* Thorofare, NJ: Slacks, Inc., 1983.

Buyse, M.L. *Birth defects encyclopedia.* Dover, MA: Center for Birth Defects Information, 1990.

Caldwell, Bettye M. & Donald J. Stedman, eds. *Infant Education: A Guide for Helping Handicapped Children in the first Three Years. First Chance Series.* New York: Walker and Co., 1977.

Cantwell, D. & Baker, L. *Developmental Speech and Language Disorders.* New York: Guilford Press, 1987.

Catts, H.W. Early Identification of dyslexia: Evidence from a follow-up study of speech-language impairment in children. *Annals of Dyslexia, 41* 163-177, 1991.

Cautela, J.R., & Groden, J. Relaxation - *A Comprehensive Manual for Adults, Children and Children with Special Needs.* Champaign, IL: Research Press, 1978.

Chrisopher, William, & Barbara Christopher. *Mixed Blessings.* Nashville: Abingdon Press, 1989.

Cipani, E. *A Guide to Developing Language Competence in Preschool Children with Severe and Moderate Handicaps.* Springfield, IL: Charles C Thomas, 1991.

Clark, L. *SOS Help for Parents: A Practical Guide for Handling Common Everyday Problems.* Bowling Green, KY: Parents Press, 1985.

Coleman, W.S. *Attention-Deficit Hyperactivity Disorder - A Handbook for Diagnosis and Treatment.* New York: Guilford Press, 1990.

Coling, Marcia Cain. *Psychological Assessment of Handicapped Children: A Guide for Parents.* Association for Retarded Citizens of Northern Virginia, 100 North Washington Street, Suite 238, Falls Church, VA 22046.

Conners, C.K. & Wells, A.C. *Hyperactive Children.* Beverly Hills: Sage, 1986.

Cooke, R.E. *Developmental Disabilities in Infancy and Childhood.* Baltimore: Paul H. Brookes, 1991.

Cowden, Jo E., L. Kristi Sayers, & Carol C. Torrey. *Pediatric Adapted Motor Development and Exercise: An Innovative, multisystem Approach for Professionals and Families.* Springfield, IL: Charles C Thomas, 1998.

Cunningham, Cliff. *Down's Syndrome: An Introduction for Parents.* London: Souvenir Press, Ltd., distributed in U.S. by Brookline Books, Inc., 1982.

Cunningham, Cliff & Patricia Sloper. *Helping Your Exceptional Baby: A Practical and Honest Approach to Raising a Mentally Handicapped Child.* New York: Pantheon Books, 1978.

Cutler, Barbara Coyne. *Unraveling the Special Education Maze: An Action Guide for Parents.* Champaign, IL: Research Press, 1981.

Dalldorf, J.S. *Autism in Adolescents and Adults.* New York: Plenum, 1983.

DeMyer, M.K. *Parents and Children in Autism.* New York: Wiley, 1979.

Des Jardins, Charlotte. *How to Get Services By Being Assertive.* Chicago: Coordinating Council for Handicapped Children, 1980.

Des Jardins, Charlotte. *How to Organize An Effective Parent/Advocacy Group and Move Bureaucracies.* Chicago: Coordinating Council for Handicapped Children, 1980.

DeVilliers, Peter A. & Jill G. De Villiers. *Early Language.* Cambridge, MA: Harvard University Press, 1979.

Dickman, Irving & Sol Gordon. *One Miracle at a Time, How to Get Help for Your Disabled Child: From the Experience of Other Parents.* New York: Simon and Schuster, 1985.

Dmitriev, Valentine. *Time to Begin: Early Education for Children with Down Syndrome.* Milton, WA: Caring, Inc., 1982.

Dodson-Burke, B., & Hill, E.W. *An Orientation and Mobility Primer for Families and Young Children.* New York: American Foundation for the Blind, 1982.

Dougan, Terrell, Lyn Isbell, & Patricia Vygas. *We Have Been There: A Guidebook for Families of People with Mental Retardation.* Nashville: Abingdon Press, 1983.

Dreifuss, Fritz E. *Pediatric Epileptology: Classification and Management of Seizures in the Child.* Littleton, MA: John Wright PSG, 1983.

Edgerton, Robert B. *Mental Retardation. The Developing Child Series.* Cambridge, MA: Harvard University Press, 1979.

Edwards, Jean & David Dawson. *My Friend David: A Sourcebook about Down's Syndrome and a Personal Story about Friendship.* Portland, OR: EDNICK Communications, Inc., 1983.

Eisenberg, M.G., Sutking, L.F. & M.A. Jansen. *Chronic Illness and Disability Through the Lifespan: Effects on Self and Family.* Vol. 4. New York: Springer, Publishing, 1984.

Featherstone, Helen. *A Difference in the Family: Life with a Disabled Child.* New York: Basic Books, 1980.

Ferrell, K.A. *Parenting Preschoolers: Suggestions for Raising Young Blind and Visually Impaired Children.* New York: American Foundation for the Blind, 1984.

Finnie, Nancie R. *Handling the Young Cerebral Palsied Child at Home.* New York: E.P. Dutton, 1975.

Fredericks, H.D. Bud. *Toilet Training the Child with Handicaps.* Monmouth, OR: Teaching Research Publications, 1975.

Friedberg, Joan Brest, June Mullins, & Adelwide Weir Sukiennik. *Accept Me As I Am: Best Books of Juvenile Nonfiction on Impairment and Disabilities.* New York: R.R. Bowler, 1985

Fuge, D.L. & Green, K.O. *Estate Planning for Retarded Persons and Their Families.* Atlanta, GA: University of Mississippi Law Center, 1982.

Gadow, Kenneth D. *Children on Medication, Volume II.* Epilepsy, Emotional Disturbance, and Adolescent Disorders. San Diego, CA: College Hill Press, 1986.

Gardner, R.J.M., & Botherland, G.R. *Chromosome Abnormalities and Genetic Counseling.* New York: Oxford University Press, 1989.

Goldberg, Sally. *Teaching with Toys: Making Your Own Educational Toys.* Ann Arbor, MI: University of Michigan Press, 1981.

Goldberg, S. *Ophthalmology Made Rediculously Simple.* Miami: MedMaster, Inc., 1989.

Goldfarb, L.A., Brotherson, M.J., Summers, J.A., & Turnbull, A.P. *Meeting the Challenge of Disability or Chronic Illness-A Family Guide.* Baltimore: Paul H. Brookes Publishing CO., 1986.

Good, Julia Darnell & Joyce Good Reis. *A Special Kind of Parenting: Meeting the Needs of Handicapped Children.* Franklin Park, IL: La Leche League International, 1985.

Gottesman, D.M. *The Powerful Parent: A Child Advocacy Handbook.* Norwalk, CT: Appleton-Century-Crofts, 1982.

Grandin, Temple, & Margaret Scariano. *Emergence: Labled Autisic.* Novato, CA: Arena Press, 1986.

Hanson, Marci J. *Teaching Your Down's Syndrome Infant: A Guide for Parents.* Baltimore: University Park Press, 1977.

Harrison, M.R., Golbus, M.S., & Filly, R.A. *The Unborn Patient: Prenatal Diagnosis and Treatment.* Philadelphia: W.B. Saunders, 1990.

Hart, C.A. *A Parent's Guide to Autism. Answers to the Most Common Questions.* New York: Pocket Books, 1993.

Healy, Alfred, Patricia D. Keesee, & Barbara S. Smith. *Early Services for Children with Special Needs: Transactions for Family Support.* Baltimore: Paul H. Brookes, 1989.

Hecker, Helen. *Travel for the Disabled: A Handbook of Travel Resources and 500 Worldwide Access Guides.* Vancouver, WA: Twin Peaks Press, 1985.

Holmes, David L. *Establsihing Group Homes for Adults with Autism.* Princeton, NJ: Eden Press, 1985.

Jablow, Martha Moraghan. *Cara: Growing with a Retarded Child.* Philadelphia: Temple University Press, 1982.

Jan, James E., Robert G. Zeigler & Guiseppe Erba. *Does Your Child Have Epilepsy?* Baltimore: University Park Press, 1983.

Johnson, Vicki M. & Roberta A. Werner. *A Step-by-Step Learning Guide for Retarded Infants and Children.* Syracuse, NY: Syracuse University Press, 1975.

Jones, Monica Loose. *Home Care for the Chronically Ill or Disabled Child.* New York: Harper and Row, 1980.

Jones, Reginald L. *Reflections on Growing Up Disabled.* Council for Exceptional Children, Association Drive, Reston, VA 22091, 1983.

Jones, S., & Clark, S. *Adaptive positioning equipment: Directory of available services.* Available from Georgia Retardation Center, 4770 North Peachtree Road, Dumwoody, GA 30338.

Kekelis, L. & Chernus-Mansfield, N. *Talk to Me: A Language Guide for Parents of Blind Children.* Los angeles, CA: Blind Childrens Center, 1984.

Kelly, J.D. (Ed.) *Recreation Programming for Visually Impaired Children and Youth.* New York: American Foundation for the Blind, 1981.

Knafl, K.L., Cavallari, K.A., & Dixon, D.M. *Pediatric Hospitalization: Family and Nurse Perpectives.* Glenview, IL: Scott, Foresman. 1988.

Koenig, A.J. & Holbrook, M.C. *The Braille Enthusiast's Directory.* Nashville, TN: SCALRS Publishing, 1995.

Koegel, R.L., Rincover, A., & Egel, A.L. *Educating and Understanding Autistic Children.* San Diego: College Hill, 1982.

Laidlaw, Mary V. & John Laidlaw. *Epilepsy Explained.* New York: Churchill Livngston, 1984.

Larson, G., & Kahn, J. *Special Needs/Special Solutions: How to Get Quality Care for a Child with Special Needs.* St. Paul, MN: Life Line Press, 1990.

Lechtenberg, Richard. *Epilepsy and the Family.* Cambridge, MA: Harvard University Press, 1984.

Letts, RM. *Principles of seating the disabled.* Ann Arbor, MI: CRC Press, 1991.

Lindemann, J.E. & Lindemann, S.J. *Growing up Proud: A Parents Guide to the Psychological Care of Children with Disabilities.* New York: Warner Books, 1988.

Lott, I.T., & McCoy, E.E. *Down Syndrome: Advances in Medical Care.* New York: Wiley-Liss, 1992.

Manes, J., & Carty, L. *SSI: New Opportunities for Children with Disabilities.* Washington, DC: Mental Health Law Projects, 1990.

McCleary, Elliot H. *Your Child Has a Future.* National Easter Seal Society, 2023 West Ogden Ave., Chicago, IL 60612.

McCollum, Audrey. *The Chronically Ill Child: A Guide for Parents and Professionals.* Boston: Brown and Co., 1981.

McMorrow, M.J., Foxx, R.M., Faw, G.D., & Bittle, R.G. *Looking for the Words— Teaching Functional Language Strategies.* Champaign, IL: Research Press, 1986.

Melton, David. *Promises to Keep: A Handbook for Parents of Learning Disabled, Brain-injured and Other Exceptional Children.* New York: Franklin Watts, 1984.

Miezio, Peggy Muller. *Parenting Children with Disabilities.* New York: Marcel Dekker, 1983.

Mulick, J.A., & Pueschel, S.M. *Parent –Professional Partnerships in Developmental Disability Services.* Cambridge, MA: Ware Press, 1983.

Mulliken, R.K., & Buckley, J.J. *Assessment of Multihandicapped and Developmentall Disabled Children.* Cambridge, MA: Aspen Systems, 1983.

Murphy, Albert T. *Special Children, Special Parents: Personal Issues with Handicapped Children.* Englewood Cliffs, NJ: Prentice-Hall, 1981.

Northern, J.L. & Downs, M.P. *Hearing in Children* (4th ed.) Baltimore: Williams and Wilkins, 1991.

Olson, M.R. & Mangold, S. *Guidelines and Games for Teaching Efficient Braille Reading.* New York: American Foundation for the Blind, 1981.

Paciorek, M.J., & Jones, A.J. *Sports and Recreation for the Disabled.* Carmel, IN: Cooper Publishing Group, 1994.

Paluszny, M. Autism: *A Practical Guide for Parents and Professionals.* Syracuse: Syracuse University Press, 1979.

Park, C.C. *The Siege–The First Eights Years of an Autistic Child.* Boston: Little, Brown, 1982.

Pearlman, L., & Scott, K.A. *Raising the Handicapped Child.* Engelwood Cliffs, NJ: Prentice Hall, 1981.

Perske, Robert. *Hope for Families: New Directions for Parents of Persons with Retardation or Other Disabilities.* Nashville: Abingdon Press, 1981.

Perske, Robert. *New Life in the Neighborhood: How Persons with Retardation or Other Disabilities Can Help Make a Good Community Better.* Nashville: Abingdon Press, 1980.

Perske, Robert, Andrew Clifton, Barbara M. Mcclean, & Jean Ishler Stein, eds. *Mealtime for Persons with Severe Handicaps.* Baltimore: Paul H. Brookes, 1986.

Powell, T.H., & Gallagher, P.A. *Brothers and Sisters–A Special Part of Exceptional Families (2nd ed.)*. Baltimore: Paul H. Brookes, 1993.

Prensky, Arthur & Helen Palkes. *Care of the Neurologically Handicapped Child*. New York: Oxford University Press, 1982.

Pueschel, S.M., ed. *The Young Child with Down Syndrome*. New York: Human Sciences Press, Inc., 1984.

Pueschel, S.M., ed. *Down Syndrome: Growing and Learning*. Kansas City: Andrews and McMell, Inc., 1978.

Pueschel, S.M. *A Parent's Guide to Down syndrome: Toward a Brighter Future*. Baltimore: Paul H. Brookes, 1990.

Roiphe, Herman & Anne Roiphe. *Your Child's Mind*. New York: St. Martin's/Marek, 1985.

Rosenfield, L.R. *Your Child and Health Care: A "Dollars and Sense" Guide for Families with Special Needs*. Baltimore: Paul H. Brookes, 1994.

Ross, Bette M. *Our Special Child: A Guide to Successful Parenting of Handicapped Children*. New York: Walker and Co., 1981.

Russell, L.M. *Alternatives: A Family Guide to Legal and Financial Planning for the Disabled*. Evanston, IL: First Publications, 1983.

Rynders, John E. & J. Margaret Horrobin. *To Give an Edge: A Guide for New Parents of Children with Down Syndrome*. St. Paul: Colwell/North Central, Inc., 1974.

Schleichkorn, Jay. *Coping with Cerebral Palsy: Answers to Questions Parents Often Ask*. Austin , TX: Pro-Ed, 1983.

Simeonsson, R.J. *Psychological and Developmental Assessment of Special Children*. Newton, MA: Allyn and Bacon, 1986.

Simmons, Robin. *After the Tears: Parents Talk about Raising a Child with a Disability*. San Diego: Harcourt Brace and Jovanovich, 1987.

Singer, G.H.S., & Powers, L.E. *Families, Disability, and Empowerment: Active Coping Skills and Strategies for Family Interventions*. Baltimore: Paul H. Brookes, 1993.

Spitainik, Deborah M. & Irving Rosentein. *All Children Grow and Learn: Activities for Parents of Children with Developmental Problems*. Temple University Developmental Disabilities Center, Ritter Annex, Philadelphia, PA 19122, 1976.

Stein, Sara Bonnett. *About Handicaps: An Open Family Book for Parents and Children Together.* New York: Walker, 1974.

Stratton, J.M. & Wright, S. *On the Way to Literacy: Early Experiences for Visually Impaired Children.* Louisville, KY: American Printing House for the Blind, 1993.

Sugarman, Gerald I. *Epilepsy Handbook: A Guide to Understanding Seizure Disorders.* St. Louis: C.V. Mosby, Company, 1984.

Sullivan, T. *Special Parents, Special Child.* New York: G.P. Putnam's Sons, 1995.

Summers, Jean Ann. *The Right to Grow Up—An Introduction to Adults with Developmental Disabilities.* Baltimore: Paul H. Brookes, 1985.

Svoboda, William B. *Learning About Epilepsy.* Baltimore: University Park Press, 1979.

Swallow, R., & Huebner, K.M. *How to Thrive, Not Just Survive: A Guide to Independent Skills for Blind and Visually Impaired Children and Youth.* Lousiville, KY: American Printing House for the Blind, 1993.

Szymanski, L.S., & Tanquay, P.E. *Emotional Disorders of Mentally Retarded Persons: Assessment, Treament, and Consultation.* Baltimore: University Park Press, 1980.

Taeusch, H.W., & Yogman, M.W. (eds.) *Follow-up Management of the High-Risk Infant.* Toronto, Ontario, Canada: Little, Brown, 1987.

Taylor, John, F. *The Hyperactive Child and Family.* New York: Dodd, Mead and Co., 1980.

Thain, Wilbur S. Glendon Castio, Ph.D. and Adrienne Peterson, R.P.T. *Normal and Handicapped Children: A Growth and Development Primer for Parents and Professionals.* Littleton, MA: PSG Publishing Co., 1980.

Thompson, Charlotte E. *Raising a Handicapped Child: A Helpful Guide for Parents of the Physically Disabled.* New York: William Morrow, 1986.

Thompson, R.J., & O'Quinn, A.N. *Developmental Sisabilities—Etiologies, Manifestations, Diagnosis, and Treatments.* New York: Oxford University Press, 1990.

Travis, G. *Chronic Illness in Children: Its Impact on Child and Family.* Stanford, CA: Standford University Press, 1976.

Tucker, B.P., & Goldstein, B.A. *Legal Rights of Persons with Disabilities.* Horsham, PA: LRP Publications, 1993.

Turecki, Stanley. *The Difficult Child.* New York, Bantam Books, 1985.

Turnbull, A.P., & Turnbull, H.R., III. *Families, Professionals, and Exceptionality–A Special Partnership.* Columbus, OH: Charles E. Merrill, 1980.

Tuttle, D., & Tuttle, N. *Self-esteem and Adjusting with Blindness.* Springfield, IL: Charles C. Thomas, 1995.

Ulrey, G., & Rogers, S.J. *Psychological Assessment of Handicapped Infants and Young Children.* New York: Thieme - Stratton, 1982.

Veen, S., Ens-Dokkum, M.H., & Schreuder, A.M. Impairments, disabilities and handicaps of very preterm and very-low-birth-weight infants of five years of age. *Lancet, 330,* 1991.

Warren, D.H. *Blindness and Children: An Individual Approach.* Cambridge: Cambridge University Press, 1994.

Wentworth, Elsie H. *Listen to Your Heart: A Message to Parents of Handicapped Children.* Boston: Houghton Mifflin, 1974.

Williamson, G.G. *Children with Spina Bifida: Early Intervention and Preschool Programming.* Baltimore: Paul H. Brookes, 1987.

Wing, L. *Autistic Children: A Guide for Parents and Professionals.* New York: Bruner/Mazel, 1985.

Wong, V.C. Cortical blindness in children: A study of etiology and prognosis. *Pediatric Neurology, 7,* 178-185, 1991.

Wyllie, E. (Ed.). *The Treatment of Epilepsy: Principles and Practice.* Philadelphia: Lea and Febiger, 1993.

Zuckerman, D., & Chrmatz, M. *Mental Disability Law–A primer: A Comprehensive Introduction to the Field.* Washington, DC: Commission on Mental and Physical Disability Law, 1992.

Education:

Anderson, Frances E. *Art-Centered Education and Education for Children with Disabilities.* Springfield, IL: Charles C Thomas, 1994.

Anderson, Frances E. *Art For All The Children: Approaches to Art Therapy for Children with Disabilities (2nd Ed).* Springfield, IL: Charles C. Thomas, 1992.

Bishop, Virginia E. *Teaching Visually Impaired Children (2nd Ed.)*. Springfield, IL: Charles C Thomas, 1996.

Blackman, H., & Peterson, D. *Totally integrated neighborhood schools*. La Grange, IL: La Grange Department of Special Education, 1989.

Blanco, Ralph F. & David F. Bogacki. *Prescriptions for Children with Learning and Adjustment Problems: A Consultant's Desk Reference*. Springfield, IL: Charles C. Thomas, 1988.

Boehm, A.E., & M.A. White. *The Parents' Handbook on School Testing*. New York: Teachers College Press, 1982.

Brigance, Albert H. and Charles H. Hargis. *Educational Assessment: Insuring That All Students Succeed in School*. Springfield, IL: Charles C Thomas, 1993.

Bruinicks, R.H., & K.C. Lakin. *Living and Learning in the Least Restrictive Environment*. Baltimore: Paul H. Brookes, 1985.

Budoff, Milton, & Alan Orenstein. *Due Process in Special Education: On Going to a Hearing*. Cambridge, MA: Brookline Books, Inc., 1982.

Burns, Edwards. *Test Accomodations for Students with Disabilities*. Springfield, IL: Charles C Thomas, 1998.

Coleman, Janet R, & Elizabeth E. Wolf. *Advanced Sign Language Vocabulary: A Resource Text for Educators, Interpreters, Parents and Sign Language Instructors*. Springfield, IL: Charles C Thomas, 1991.

Cutler, Barbara Coyne. *Unraveling the Special Education Maze: An Action Guide for Parents*. Champaign, IL: Research Press, 1981.

Davis, Kimberly. *Adapted Physical Education for Students with Autism*. Springfield, IL: Charles C Thomas, 1990.

Duran, Elva. Teaching Students with Moderate/Severe Disabilities, Including Autism: Strategies for Second Language Learners in Inclusive Settings (2nd Ed). Springfield, IL: Charles C Thomas, 1996.

Fairchild, Thomas N. *Crisis Intervention Strategies for School-Based Helpers*. Springfield, IL: Charles C Thomas, 1997.

Fine, Aubrey H. & Nya M. Fine. *Therapeutic Recreation for Exceptional Children: Let Me In, I Want to Play (2nd Ed)*. Springfield, IL: Charles C Thomas, 1996.

Grabow, Beverly W. *Your Child Has A Learning Disability–What Is It?* Chicago: National Easter Seal Society, 1978.

Greene, Lawrence J. *Learning Disabilities and Your Child: A Survival Handbook.* New York: Ballantine Books, 1987.

Handleman, J.S., & Harris, S.L. *Educating the Developmentally Disabled: Meeting the Needs of Children and Families.* San Diego: College Hill, 1986.

Hart, V. *Maistreaming Children with Special Needs.* New York: Longman, 1980.

Harley, Randall K., Mila B. Truan, & LaRhea D. Sanford. *Communication Skills for Visually Impaired Learners: Braille, Print, and Listening Skills for Students Who are Visually Impaired (2nd Ed).* Springfield, IL: Charles C Thomas, 1997.

Hollis, James N. *Conducting Individualized Education Program Meetings That Withstand Due Process: The Informal Evidentiary Proceeding.* Springfield, IL: Charles C Thomas, 1998.

Jones, Carroll J. *Social And Emotional Development of Exceptional Students: Handicapped and Gifted.* Springfield, IL: Charles C Thomas, 1992.

Lerner, Janet. *Learning Disabilities (3rd Ed).* Boston: Houghton Mifflin Co., 1981

Levine, M. *Keeping A Head in School: Students Book About Learning Abilities and Learning disorders.* Cambridge, MA: Educator's Publishing Service, 1990.

Lillie, David L., & Patricia A.Place. *Partners: A guide to Working with Schools for Parents of Children with Special Instructional Needs.* Glenview, IL: Scott, Foresman, 1982.

Lombana, Judy H. *Guidance for Students with Disabilities.* Springfield, IL: Charles C Thomas, 1992.

Love, Harold D. *Assessment of Intelligence and Development of Infants and Young Children: With Specialized Measures.* Springfield, IL: Charles C Thomas, 1991.

Love, Harold D. *Psychological Evaluation of Exceptional Children.* Springfield, IL: Charles C Thomas, 1985.

Love, Harold D. *Characteristics of the Mildly Handicapped: Assisting Teachers, Counselors, Psychologists, and Families to Prepare for Their Roles in Meeting the Needs of the Mildly Handicapped in a Changing Society.* Springfield, IL: Charles C Thomas, 1997.

Milgram, Roberta M. *Teaching Gifted and Talented Learners in Regular Classrooms.* Springfield, IL: Charles C. Thomas, 1989.

Michael, Robert J. *The Educator's Guide to Students with Epilepsy.* Springfield, IL: Charles C Thomas, 1995.

Mopsik, Stanley, & Judith A. Argard, eds. *An Education Handbook for Parents of Handicapped Children.* Cambridge, MA: Brookline Books, 1985.

Morgan, D.P. *A Primer on Individualized Education Programs for Exceptional Children.* Reston, VA: Council for Exceptional Children, 1981.

Nevil, Nevalyn F., Marna L. Beatty, & David P. Moxley. *Socialization Games For Persons With Disabilities: Structured Group Activities for Social and Interpersonal Development.* Springfield, IL: Charles C Thomas, 1997.

Parker, H.C. *The ADD Hyperactivity Handbook for Schools.* Plantation, FL: Impact Publications, 1992.

Parker, H.C. *The ADD Hyperactivity Workbook for Parents, Teachers and Kids.* Plantation, FL: Impact Publications, 1990.

Plumridge, Diane M., Robin Bennett, Nuhad Dinno, & Cynthia Branson. *The Student With A Genetic Disorder: Educational Implications for Special Education Teachers and for Physical Therapists, Occupational Therapists, and Speech Pathologists.* Springfield, IL: Charles C Thomas, 1993.

Pollack, Doreen, Donald Goldberg, & Nancy Coleffe-Schenck. *Educational Audiology for the Limited-Hearing Infant and Preschooler: An Auditory-Verbal Program.* (3rd Ed.) Springfield, IL: Charles C Thomas, 1997.

Roweley-Kelly, F.L., & Reigel, D.H. (Eds.) *Teaching the Student with Spina Bifida.* Baltimore: Paul Brookes, 1993.

Rubin, Phyliss, & Jeanine Tregay. *Play with Them—Theraplay Groups in the Classroom: A Technique for Professionals Who Work with Children.* Springfield, IL: Charles C Thomas, 1989.

Schimmel, David, & Louis Fischer. *Parents, Schools and the Law.* Columbia, MD: The National Committee for Citizens in Education, 1987.

Shrybman, James A. *Due Process in Special Education.* Rockville, MD: Aspen Publications, 1982.

Silver, L. *The Misunderstood Child: A Guide for Parents of Learning Disabled Children.* New York: McGraw-Hill, 1984

Smith, Sally L. *No Easy Answers: The Learning Disabled Child at Home and at School.* New York: Bantam, 1981

Sternberg, Les, Ronald L. Taylor, & Steven C. Russell. *Negotiating the Disability Maze: Critical Knowledge for Parents, Professionals, and Other Caring Persons (2nd Ed)*. Springfield, IL: Charles C Thomas, 1996.

Swanson, Merylyn S. *At-Risk Students in Elementary Education: Effective Schools for Disadvantaged Learners*. Springfield, IL: Charles C Thomas, 1991.

Treif, Ellen. *Working With Visually Impaired Young Students: A Curriculum Guide for Birth-3 Year Olds*. Springfield, IL: Charles C Thomas, 1992.

Treif, Ellen. *Working with Visually Impaired Young Students: A Curriculum Guide for 3 to 5 Year Olds*. Springfield, IL: Charles C Thomas, 1998.

Walsh, William M., & G. Robert Williams. *Schools and Family Therapy: Using Systems Theory and Family Therapy in the Resolution of School Problems*. Springfield, IL: Charles C Thomas, 1997.

Childhood Mental Disability:

Apter, Steven J., & Jane Close Conoley. *Childhood Behavior Disorders and Emotional Disturbances*. Englewood Cliffs, NJ: Prentice-Hall, 1984.

Apter, Steven J. *Troubled Children: Troubled Systems*. New York: Pergamon Press, 1982.

Binkard, Betty, Marge Goldberg, & Paula F. Goldberg. *A Guidebook for Parents of Children with Emotional Disorders*. Minneapolis, MN: Pacer Center, Inc., 1984.

Cantor, Sheila. *The Schizophrenic Child: A Primer for Parents and Professionals*. Toronto: The University of Toronto Press, 1982.

Gattozzi, Ruth. *What's Wrong with My Child?* New York: McGraw-Hill, 1986.

Giovacchini, Peter. *The Urge to Die: Why Young People Commit Suicide*. New York: Macmillan, 1981.

Hafen, Brent Q., & Kathryn J. Frandsen. *Youth Suicide: Depression and Loneliness*. Evergreen, CO: Cordillera Press, 1986.

Hatfield, Agnes. *Coping with Mental Illness in the Family: A Family Guide*. National Alliance for the Mentally Ill, 1984.

Kaufman, J.M. *Characteristics of Children's Behavior Disorders*. Columbus, OH: Charles E. Merrill, 1981.

McCoy, Kathleen. *Coping with Teenage Depression: A Parent's Guide*. New York: New American Library, 1982.

McDowell, Richard L., Gary W. Adamson, & Frank H. Wood. *Teaching Emotionally Disturbed Children.* Boston: Little, Brown and Company, 1982.

McKnew, Donald, Leon Cytryn, & Herbert Yahraes. *Why Isn't Johnny Crying? Coping with Depression in Children.* New York: W.W. Norton and Co., 1983.

Morrison, James. *Your Brother's Keeper: A Guide for Families of the Mentally Ill.* Chicago: Nelson-Hall, 1981.

Torrey, E. Fuller. *Surviving Schizophrenia: A Family Manual.* New York: Harper and Row, 1983.

MULTIMEDIA RESOURCES

Videos:

Autism Video Series. Princeton, NJ: Films for the Humanities.

Barkley, R. ADHD–What Can We Do? New York: Guilford, 1992

Barkley, R. ADHD–What Do We Know? New York: Guilford, 1992

"Being with people: Social Skills training for persons with special needs." Champaign, IL: Research Press.

BFA Low Cost Videos. St. Louis: BFA Educational Media.

Copeland, E.D. "ADHD/ADD video resource for schools–Attention disorders: The school's vital role." Port Chester, NY: National Professional Resources, 1989.

Disabilities and Special Education Film and Video Rental Service. Bloomington, IN: Indiana University Audio Visual Center.

DVS Home Videos. St. Paul, MN: DVS Home Video. Descriptive Video Service for visually impaired.

"Educating Peter." Port Chester, New York: National Professional Resources, Inc., 1992.

Educational Activities Video, Multimedia, and Software. Baldwin, NY: Educational Activities, Inc.

An Exceptional Child Video Series. Princeton, NJ: Films for the Humanities, Inc.

Goldstein, S., and Goldstein, M. Educating Inattentive Children. Salt Lake City, UT: Neurology Learning & Behavior Center, 1990.

Goldstein, S., and Goldstein, M. It's Just Attention Disorder. Salt Lake City, UT: Neurology Learning and Behavior Center, 1989.

Hearing and Speech Video Series. Princeton, NY: Films for the Humanities.

Living with Disabilities. Chicago: Society for Visual Education. Series of films and tapes presenting children with disabilities.Disabilities presented: Down syndrome, cerebral palsy, epilepsy, hearing and visual impairment and spina bifida.

Morse, W., & J. Smith. Understanding Child Variance Video Tape Series. Reston, VA: Council of Exceptional Children.

"Nonviolent crisis intervention for the educator: Volume I: The disruptive child; VolumeII: The disruptive adolescent; VolumeIII: The assaultive student." Brookfield, WI: National Crisis Prevention Institute.

NPR Videos. Port Chester NY: National Professional Resources. Videos on ADD and thinking skills.

"Oh, I see." New York, NY: Amercian Foundation for the Blind.

Phelan, T. Attention Deficit Hyperactivity Disorder (two-part video and book). Glen Ellyn, IL: Child Management, Inc., 1990.

"Somedays' child: A Focus on special needs children and their families." Portland, OR: Educational Productions.

Strategies for Training Regular Educators to Teach Children with Handicaps (STRETCH). Northbrook, IL: Hubbard.

"Teaching mildly handicapped students: Video training in effective instruction." Reston, VA: Council of Exceptional Children.

Teaching People with Developmental Disabilities. Champaign, IL: Research Press.

"Teaching the student with spina bifida videotape" Baltimore: Paul H. Brookes. Companion to book by same title.

Variety Preschoolers' Workshop Videos. Syosset, NY: Variety Preschoolers' Workshop. Focuses on preschoolers with special needs.

Audio Cassettes:

The following offer catalogues featuring a variety of tapes for parents.

B.L. Winch and Associates, 45 Hitching Post Drive, Bldg. 2, Rolling Hills Estates, CA 90274. 800-662-9662

General Cassette Corp. 602-269-3111

Marko Enterprises, 1831 Fort Union Blvd., Salt Lake City, UT 84121.

Nightengale-Conant Corp. 1-800-323-5552.

Psychology Today Tapes, 1-800-345-8112.

Magazines, Journals and Newsletters:

Advocate. The Autism Society of America, 1234 Massachusetts Ave., NW, Ste. 1017, Washington, D.C. 20005.

The ARC. Association of Retarded Citizens of the U.S., 2051 Avenue J, Arlington, TX 76006. 817-640-0204

Augmentive Communication News. One Surf Way, Ste. 215, Monterey, CA 93940.

Closing the Gap. P.O. Box 68, Henderson, MN 56044. 612-248-3294
Newsletter featuring microcomputer technology for persons with severe disabilities.

Disabled U.S.A. President's Committee on Employment of the Handicapped, 1111 20th St., N.W., 6th Fl., Washington, DC 20036.

Especially Grandparents. King County ARC, 2230 Eighth Ave., Seattle, WA 98121.

Exceptional Parent. 605 Commonwealth Ave., Boston, MA 02215.617-526-8961

Network News. National Network of Parents Centers, 312 Stuart St., 2nd Fl., Boston, MA 02116. Educational advocacy issues.

Newlsetter. NICHY, Box 1492, Washington, DC 20013. For people who work or live with people who have special needs.

OSERS News in Print. Office of Special Education and Rehabilitative Services, 330 C St., SW, 3018 Switzer Bldg. Washington, DC 20202.

Pacesetter Newsletter. Parent Advocacy Coalition for Educational Rights (PACER), 4826 Chicago Ave., Minneapolis, MN 55417.

Sibling Information Network Newsletter. Connecticut's University Affiliated Program, School of Education, The University of Connecticut, Box U-64, Room 227, Storrs, CT 06268.

Computer Software:

The following is a list of companies who supply software for children with special needs. Most provide catalogues.

Academic Software, Inc. 331 W. 2nd St. at Broadway, Lexington, KY 40507. 606-233-2332

Academic Therapy Publications. 20 Commercial Blvd., Novato, CA 94947. 415-883-3314

Access Unlimited. 3535 Briarpark Dr., Ste. 102, Houston, TX 77042-5235. 800-848-0311

ACS Software. University of WA, Dept. of Speech and Hearing Sciences JG-15, Seattle, WA 98195. 206-543-7974

Advanced Ideas Inc. 680 Hawthorne Dr. Tibourn, CA 94024. 415-425-5086

Ahead Designs. 1827 Hawk View Dr., Encinitas, CA 92024. 619-942-5860

Al Squared. 1463 Hearst Dr., Atlanta, GA 30319. 404-233-7065

American Guidance Services. Publisher's Bldg. Circle Pines, MN 56223. 800-328-2560

American Printing House for the Blind. P.O. Box 6085, Louisville, KY 40206-0085. 502-895-2405

Amidon Publications. 1966 Benson Ave. St. Paul, MN 56116. 800-328-6502

Aquaris Instructional. P.O. Box 819, Indian Rocks Beach, FL 34635. 800-338-2644

Arkenstone, Inc. 1185 Bordeaux Dr., Ste. D, Sunnyvale, CA 94089. 800-444-4443

BrainTrain, Inc. 727 Twin Ridge Lane, Richmond, VA 23235. 800-446-5456

Bright Star Technology, Inc. 1450 114th Ave. SE., Ste. 200, Bellevue, WA 98044. 206-451-3697

Broderbund Software, Inc. 500 Redwood Blvd., P.O. Box 6121, Novato, CA 94958-6121. 800-521-6263

Cambridge Developmental Laboratory Special Times Education Software. 86 West Street, Waltham, MA 02154. 800-637-0047

Castle Special Computer Services, Inc. 9801 San Gabriel NE, Albuquerque, NM. 87111-3530. 505-293-8379

CLASS Adaptive Technologies. 16 Haverhill St., Andover, MA 01810.

Communication Skill Builders. P.O. Box 42050, Tucson, AZ 85733. 603-323-7500

ComputAbility Corp. 40000 Grand River, Ste. 109, Novi, MI 48375. 313-477-6720

Compu-Teach. 14924 21st Dr. SE, Mill Creek, WA 98012. 800-448-3224

Computer Tutor, Inc. 1001 15th Pl., Plano, TX 75704. 800-472-0071

Computers to Help People, Inc. 1221 W. Johnson St., Madison, WI 53715-1046. 608-257-5917

Creative Learning, Inc. P.O. Box 829, North San Juan, CA 95960. 800-842-5360

Cross Educational Software. 504 E. Kentucky Ave., P.O. Box 1536, Ruston, LA 71270. 318-255-8921

Curriculum Associates, Inc. 5 Esquire Rd., North Billerica, MA 08162. 508-667-8000

DLM Teaching Resources. One DLM Park. Allen, TX 75002. 800-527-5030

Easter Seals & Lehigh Valley Computer Project. P.O. Box 333, 1161 Forty Foot Rd., Kulpsville, PA 19443. 215-866-8092

Exceptional Children's Software. P.O. Box 487, Hays, KY 67601. 913-625-9281

Gameco Industries: Materials for the Exceptional Student. P.O. Box 310 R23, Big Spring, TX 79721-1911. 800-351-1404

Growing Minds Software. P.O. Box 3704, Ontario, CA 91761-0791. 714-391-2252

Houghton Mifflin School Division. One Memorial Dr., Cambridge, MA 02178. 800-992-5121

Humanities Software. P.O. Box 950, Hood River, OR 97031. 800-245-6737

IBM Educational Systems. P.O. Box 2150, Atlanta, GA 30301-2150. 800-426-2133 or 800-284-9482 TDD

Institut Nazareth et Louis Braille. 1111, St-Charles ouest, Longueil, PQJ4K 5G4 Canada 514-463-1710

Kidsview Software. P.O. Box 98, Warner, NH 03278. 603-927-4428

KidTech. 21274 Oak Knoll, Tehachapi, CA 93561. 805-822-1633

Milliken Publishing Co. P.O. Box 21579, 1100 Research Blvd., St. Louis, MO 63132. 314-991-4220

Society for Visual Education, Inc. 1345 Diversey Pkwy., Chicago, IL 60614. 800-829-1900

Sunburst Communication. 39 Washington Ave., Pleasantville, NY 10570. 800-628-8897

TASH Inc. (Technical Aids & Systems for the Handicapped). 70 Gibson Dr., Unit 12 Markhan, ON L3R 4C2 Canada. 416-475-2212

Teacher Support Software. 1035 NW 57th St.m Gainesville, FL 32605. 800-228-2871

Technology for Language and Learning. P.O. Box 327, East Rockway, NY 11518-0327. 516-625-4550

Trace Research and Development Center. Rm. S-151 Waisman Ctr., 1500 Highland Ave., University of Wisconsin, Madison, WI 53705. 608-262-6966

UCLA Intervention Program for Handicapped Children. 1000 Veteran Ave., Rm. 23-10, Los Angeles, CA 90024. 301-825-4821

Vocational and Rehabilitation Research Institute. 3304 33rd St. NW, Calgary, AB T2L 2A6 Canada. 403-284-1121

Vysion, Inc. 30777 Schoolcraft Rd. Livonia, MI 48150. 800-521-1350

Wings for Learning, Inc. 1600 Green Hills Rd., P.O. Box 660002, Scotts Valley, CA 95067-0002. 800-321-7511

Words+, Inc. P.O. Box 1229, Lancaster, CA 93584. 800-869-8521

RESOURCES FOR ADAPTIVE EQUIPMENT,
TOYS AND CLOTHING

Adaptive Equipment:

Equipment Shop
P.O. Box 33
Bedford, MA 01730
617-275-7681
Offers strollers, seats, prone standers, etc.

Kaye Products Inc.
535 Dimmocks Mill Rd.
Hillsborough, NC 27278
919-732-6444
Adaptive equipment and therapy products.

Ortho-Kinetics
P.O. Box 1647
Waukesha, WI 53187
800-824-1068
Prone standers, travel chairs, bath seats and other adaptive equipment.

J.A. Preston Corporation
60 Page Rd.
Clifton, NJ 07012
800-631-7277
Adaptive equipment and toys.

Rifton
Equipment for the Handicapped
Route 213
Rifton, NY 12471
914-658-3141
Infant and toddler chairs, bath and shower seats, swings, wedges, adaptive tables, rolls and toys.

Wheelchair Manufacturers:

ETAC USA, Inc.
3233 West Mission Oaks Blvd.
Parkland Drive, Ste. P
Camarillo, CA 93012
800-678-3822

Everest & Jennings
2325 Parklawn Drive,
Waukesha, WI 53186
805-987-6911

Sunrise Medical Quickie Designs
2842 Business Park Ave.
Fresno, CA 93727
209-292-2171

Wheelring, Inc.
199 Forst Street
Manchester, CT 06040
203-647-8596

Technical Equipment

AT&T National Special Needs Center
800-233-1222
Offers telephone related devices for people with special needs.

Toys:

Hals Pals
P.O. Box 3490
Winter Park, CO 80482

Kaye's Kids
1010 E. Pettigrew Street
Durham, NC 27701-4299
919-683-1051

The Nintendo Hands-Free Controller
800-422-2602

Salco
1145 150th Street East
Nerstrand, MN 55053
507-645-8720

Toys for Special Children
385 Warburton Avenue
Hastings, NY 10706
914-478-0960

Clothing:

Special Clothes
P.O. Box 4220
Alexandria, VA 22303
703-683-7343

Exceptionally Yours
60 Joseph Road
P.O. Box 3246
Farmingham, MA 01701
508-877-9757

Catalogues Offering More Assistive Services:

Church, G., & Glennen, S. *The Handbook of Assistive Devices.* San Diego, CA: Singular, 1992.

Danmar Products, Inc. 2390 Winewood, Ann Arbor, MI 48103. Catalogue offering adaptive equipment, headgear, swimming and positioning aids and toys.

Directory of Information Resources for the Handicapped: A Comprehensive Guide to Information Resources and Sources for the Handicapped. Santa Monica, CA: Ready Reference Press, 1980.

Durgin, Rod W., Linsay, Norene, & Hamilton, Ellen. *The Guide to Recreation, Leisure and Travel for the Handicapped. Volume I: Recreation and Sports.* Toledo, OH: Resource Directories, 1985. Also a resource on toys and crafts for children with special needs.

Jones, S. & Clark, S. *Adaptive Positioning Equipment: Directory of Available Services.* Available from Georgia Retardation Center, 4770 North Peachtree Road, Dumwoody, GA 30338.

Katz, A.H., & K. Martin. *Handbook of Services for the Handicapped.* Westport, CT: Greenwood Press, 1982. Offers resources for housing, financial aid, vocational rehabilitation, recreation, physical care, and other special services.

Slovak, Irene, *BOSC Directory.* Facilities for Learning Disabled People. Conger, NY: BOSC publishers, 1985. State-by-state resources for independent living programs and schools.

ADOPTION RESOURCES

National Organizations:

AASK America/Adopt a Special Kid
657 Mission St., Ste. 303
San Francisco, CA 94105
415-543-2275 or 800-232-2751

Adoption Exchange Association
925 Niagara St., Ste. 303
Denver, CO 80224
303-333-0845

Adoptive Families of America
333 Hwy. 100 N
Minneapolis, MN 55422
612-535-4829

American Adoption Congress
100 Connecticut Ave., NW, Ste. 9
Washington, DC 20036
800-274-6736

American Bar Association
Center on Children and the Law
1800 M St. NW, Ste. 300 S
Washington, DC 20036
202-331-2250

American Public Welfare Association
810 First St., NE
Washington, DC 20002-4205
202-682-0100

Children Awaiting Parents, Inc.
700 Exchange St.
Rochester, NY 14608
716-2332-5110

Child Welfare Institute
1365 Peachtree St., NE, Ste. 700
Atlanta, GA 30309
404-876-1934

Child Welfare League of America
440 First St., NW, Ste. 310
Washington, DC 20001
202-638-2952

Committee for Single Adoptive Parents, Inc.
P.O. Box 15084
Chevy Chase, MD 20825

Musser Foundation
1105 Cape Coral Pkwy.
Cape Coral, FL 33904
800-447-7335

National Adoption Center
1500 Walnut St., Ste. 701
Philadelphia, PA 19102
1-800-TO-ADOPT or 215-735-9988

National Adoption Information Clearinghouse
Cygnus Corporation
11426 Rockville, Pike, Ste. 410
Rockville, MD 20852

National Committee for Adoption
1930 17th St.m NW
Washington, DC 20009
202-328-1200

National Federation for Open Adoption Education
391 Taylor Blvd., Ste. 100
Pleasant Hill, CA 94523
510-827-2229

National Foster Parent Association
C/O 226 Kilts Dr.
Houston, TX 77024

National Resource Center for Special Needs Adoption
16250 Northland Dr., Ste. 120
Southfield, MI 48705
313-443-7080

North American Council on Adoptable Children
1821 University Ave., Ste. N-498
St. Paul, MN 55104
612-644-3036

Post Adoption Center for Education and Research
2255 Ygnacio Valley Rd.
Walnut Creek, CA 94598
415-935-6622

Regional Exchanges:

AASK Midwest
1025 N Reynolds Rd., Ste. 201
Toledo, OH 43615
419-534-4450
Covers Illinois, Indiana, Iowa, Michigan, Minnesota, Ohio, Wisconsin.

Adoption Center of Delaware Valley
1500 Walnut St., Ste. 701
Philadelphia, PA 19102
800-TO-ADOPT or 215-735-9988
Covers Delaware, District of Columbia, Maryland, New Jersey, Pennsylvania, Virginia, West Virginia.

Massachusetts Adoption Resource Exchange, Inc.
867 Boylston St.
Boston, MA 02116
617-536-0362
Covers Connecticut, Maine, Massachussets, New Hampshire, Rhode Island, Vermont.

Northwest Adoption Exchange
909 NE 43rd St., Ste. 208
Seattle, WA 98105
206-632-1480
Covers Alaska, Idaho, Nevada, Oregon, Utah, Washington.

Rocky Mountain Adoption Exchange
925 Niagara St., Ste. 100
Denver, CO 80224
303-333-0845
Covers Colorado, Nevada, New Mexico, South Dakota, Utah, Wyoming.

SouthEastern Exchange of the United States
P.O. Box 6647
Columbia, SC 29260-6647
803-782-0082
Covers Alabama, Florida, Georgia, Kentuckey, Mississippi, North Carolina, South Carolina, Tennessee.

Three Rivers Adoption Council
307 4th Ave., Ste. 710
Pittsburgh, PA 15222
412-471-8722
Covers Delaware, District of Columbia, Maryland, New Jersey, Pennsylvania, Virginia, West Virginia.
Tri-State Adoption Exchange
Department of Human Services
221 State St.
Augusta, ME 04333
207-289-2971
Covers Maine, New Hampshire, Vermont.

Magazines and Newsletters:

Add-Option
Aid to Adoption of Special Kids
657 Mission St., Ste. 601
San Francisco, CA 94105

Adoptalk
North American Council on Adoptable Children
1821 University Ave., Ste. N-498
St. Paul, MN 55104

Adopted Child Newsletter
P.O. Box 9362
Moscow, ID 83843

The Adoption Advocate's NEWSletter
Adoption Advocate's Press
1921 Ohio St, NE Ste. 5
Palm Bay, FL 32907

Adoptive Families of America
333 Hwy, 110 N
Minneapolis, MN 55422

AdoptNet Magazine
P.O. Box 50514
Palo Alto, CA 94303-9998

The Decree
American Adoption Congress
100 Connecticut Ave., NW, Ste. 9
Washington, DC 20036
800-274-6736

FACE Facts
Families Adopting Children Everywhere
P.O. Box 28058 Northwood Station
Baltimore, MD 21239

Root and Wings
15 Nancy Terrace
Hackettstown, NJ 07840

RESOURCES FOR CHILDREN'S BOOKS

Adoption Book Catalog
Tapestry Books
P.O. Box 359
Ringoes, NJ 08551-0359
800-765-2367

Adoptive Families of America Resources
3333 Highway 100 N
Minneapolis, MN 554221
800-372-3300

Friedberg, J.B., Mullins, J.B., & Sukiennik, A.W. *Portraying Persons with Disabilities: An Annotated Bibliography of Nonfiction for Children and Teenagers.* New Providence, NJ: R.R. Bowker, 1991.

Magination Press Books for Children. New York, NY: Magination Press Books. Specializes in picture books about the therapy process. For families and children with special needs.

Moulton, G., & Van Der Voo, A. Insight Books. San Diego: Wright Group. A series of 12 illustrated books for young children. Topics covered are developmental disabilities.

Robertson, D. *Portraying Persons with Disabilities: An Annotated Bibliography of Fiction for Children and Teenagers.* New Providence, NJ: R.R. Bowker, 1992.

Wilmor Distribution Center Books. Williamsport, PA: Wilmor. Offers a variety of children's books from many different publishing houses. Most cover children with developmental disabilities.

STATE-BY-STATE LISTING OF ADOPTION, SPECIAL EDUCATION, AND PUBLIC AND PRIVATE AGENCIES ASSISTING CHILDREN WITH SPECIAL NEEDS

Alabama:

State Department of Human Resources
50 Ripley Street
Montgomery, AL 36130
205-242-9500

Director of Special Education
Student Instructional Services
State Department of Education
1020 Monticello Court
Montgomery, AL 36117-1901
205-261-5099

Program Director
Alabama Disabilities Advocacy Program
P.O. Drawer 2847
Tuscaloosa, AL 35487-2847
205-348-4928

Director- Rehabilitation & Crippled Children Service
P.O. Box 11586
Montgomery, AL 36111-0586
205-281-8780

Special Education Action Committee
P.O. Box 161274
Mobile, AL 36606
205-478-1208

Alaska:

Department of Health & Social Services, Division of Family and Youth Services
P.O. Box H
Juneau, AK 99811-0630
907-465-3633

Director of Special Education
Office of Special Services
Alaska Department of Education
P.O. Box F
Juneau, AK 99811
907-465-2970

Director-Advocacy Services of Alaska
325 E 3rd Avenue, 2nd floor
Anchorage, AK 99501
907-273-3658

Director-Division of Vocational Rehabilitation
Pouch F, MS 0581
Juneau, AK 9981
907-465-2814

Arizona:

Department of Economic Security
P.O. Box 6123
Site Code 940 A
Phoenix, AZ 85005
602-542-2362

Director of Special Education
Special Education Section
Department of Education
1535 W Jefferson
Phoenix, AZ 85007-3280
602-255-3183

Protection & Advocacy
Arizona Center for Law in the Public Interest
112 N. Central Ave., Ste. 400
Phoenix, AZ 85004
602-252-4904

Administrator-Rehabilitative Services Administration
1300 W Washington St.
Phoenix, AZ 85007
602-255-3332

Pilot Parents
2005 N. Central Avenue #100
Phoenix, AZ 85004
602-271-4012

Arkansas:

Department of Human Services
Division of Children and Family Services
P.O. Box 1437
Little Rock, AR 72203
501-682-8345

Director of Special Education
Special Education Section
Arkansas Department of Education
Education Bldg., Room 105-C
#4 Capitol Mall
Little Rock, AR 72201
501-371-2161

Director—Advocacy Services, Inc.
Medical Arts Bldg., Ste. 311
12th & Marshall Streets
Little Rock, AR 72202

Commissioner
Arkansas Dept. of Human Services
Rehabilition Services Division
P.O. Box 3781
Little Rock, AR 72203

Arkansas Coalition for the Handicapped
519 E Fifth Street
Little Rock, AR 72202
501-376-3420

FOCUS
2917 King Street, Ste. C
Jonesboro, AR 72401
501-935-2750

California:

Adoptions Branch
Department of Social Services
744 P Street
Sacramento, CA 95814
916-322-3778

Director of Special Education
Specialized Programs Branch
Special Education Division
P.O. Box 844272
Sacramento, CA 94244-2720
916-323-4768

Executive Director
Protection & Advocacy, Inc.
2131 Capitol Ave., Ste. 100
Sacramento, CA 95816
916-447-3327 or 800-952-5746

Director—Dept. of Rehabilitation
830 K St. Mall
Sacramento, CA 95814
916-445-3971

Team of Advocates for Special Education (TASK)
18685 Santa Ynez
Fountain Valley, CA 92708
714-962-6332

Parents Helping Parents
535 Race St., Ste. 220
San Jose, CA 95126
408-288-5010

Colorado:

Dept. of Social Services
1575 Sherman Street
Denver, CO 80203-1714
303-866-3209 or 303-866-3228

Director of Special Education
Special Education Services Unit
Colorado Dept. of Education
201 E Colfax
Denver, CO 90203
303-866-6694

Director–The Legal Center
455 Sherman St., Ste. 130
Denver, CO 80203
303-722-0300

Director–Division of Rehabilitation
Dept. of Social Services
1575 Sherman St., 4th Floor
Denver, CO 80203

Parent Education and Assistance for Kids (PEAK)
6055 Lehman Drive, Ste. 101
Colorado Springs, CO 80918
719-531-9400 or 800-621-8386 ext.338 (in Colorado)

Connecticut:

Department of Children & Youth Services
Connecticut Resource Exchange
Whitehall Bldg. 2
Undercliff Road
Meriden, CT 06450
203-238-6640

Director of Special Education
Bureau of Special Education and Pupil Personnel Services
P.O. Box 2219
Hartford, CT 06102-2219
203-566-3561

Director-Office of Protection & Advocacy for Handicapped
& Developmentally Disabled Persons
90 Washington St.
Hartford, CT 06106
203-566-7616 ext.2102 or 800-842-7303 (in Connecticut)

Associate Commissioner
State Department of Education
Division of Vocational Rehabilitation
600 Asylum Ave.
Hartford, CT 06105
203-666-4440

Connecticut Parent Advocacy Center, Inc.
P.O. Box 579
East Lyme, CT 06333
203-739-3089 or 800-445-CPAL (in Connecticut)

Delaware:

Adoption Services
1825 Faulkland Road
Wilmington, DE 19805-1195
302-633-2655

Director of Special Education
Exceptional Children/Special Programs Division
Department of Public Instruction
P.O. Box 1402
Dover, DE 19903
302-736-5471

Administrator–Disabilities Law Program
144 E Market St.
Georgetown, DE 19947
302-856-0038

Director–Division of Vocational Rehabilitation
Department of Labor
State Office Bldg., 7th Floor
820 French St.
Wilmington, DE
302-571-2850

Parent Information Center of Delaware, Inc.
325 E Main Street, Ste. 203
Newark, NJ 19711
302-366-0152

District of Columbia:

Department of Human Services
609 H Street NE
Washington, DC 20002
202-727-7226

Director of Special Education
Division of Special Education and Pupil Personnel Services
DC Public Schools
Webster Administration Bldg.
10th & H Streets, NW
Washington, DC 20001
202-724-4018

Director—nformation, Protection, & Advocacy Center for
Handicapped Individuals, Inc.
300 eye St., NE, Ste. 202
Washington, DC 20002

Administrator—DC Rehabilitation Services Administration
Commission on Social Services
Department of Human Services
605 G St., NW, Room 1101
Washington, DC 20001
202-727-3227

Florida:

Department of Health & Rehabilitative Services, Children, Youth, and Families
1317 Winewood Blvd.
Tallahassee, FL 32399-0700
904-488-8000

Director of Special Education
Bureau of Education for Exceptional Studies
Florida Department of Education, Knott Building
Tallahassee, FL 32301
904-488-1570

Director—Advocacy Center for Persons with Disabilities, Inc.
2661 Executive Center Circle, W
209 Clifton Bldg.
Tallahassee, FL 32301
904-488-9070 or 800-342-0823 (TDD)

Director—Division of Vocational Rehabilitation
1709-A Mahan Dr.
Tallahassee, FL 32399-0696
904-488-6210

Parent Education Network of Florida, Inc.
2215 East Henry Avenue
Tampa, FL 33601
813-238-6100

Georgia:

State Adoption Unit
878 Peachtree Street NE
Atlanta, GA 30309
404-894-4454

Director of Special Education
Program for Exceptional Children
Georgia Department of Education
1970 Twin Towers East
205 Butler Street
Atlanta, GA 30334-1601
404-656-2425

Director—Georgia Advocacy Office, Inc.
1447 Peachtree St., NE, Ste. 811
Atlanta, GA 30309
404-885-1447 or 800-282-4538 (in Georgia)

Director-Division of Rehabilitative Services
Department of Human Services
878 Peachtree St., NE, Room 706
Atlanta, GA 30309
404-894-6670

Parents Educating Parents
Georgia ARC
1851 Ram Runway, Ste. 104
College Park, GA 30337
404-761-2745

Hawaii:

Department of Human Services
Family & Adult Services Division
420 Waiakamilo Business Center
Waiakamilo Road, Ste. 113
Honolulu, HI 96817
808-832-5151

Director of Special Education
Special Needs Branch
State Department of Education
3430 Leahi Avenue
Honolulu, HI 96815
808-737-3720

Director–Protection & Advocacy Agency of Hawaii
1580 Makoloa St., Ste. 1060
Honolulu, HI 96814
808-949-2922

Administrator–Division of Vocational Rehabilitation &
Services for the Blind
Department of Social Services
P.O. Box 339
Honolulu, HI 96809
808-548-4769

Idaho:

Adoptions, Division of Family & Children's Services
Department of Health & Welfare
450 West State Street
Boise, ID 83720
208-334-5700

Director of Special Education
State Department of Education
650 W State Street
Boise, ID 83720-0001
208-334-3940

Idaho's Coalition of Advocates for the Disabled, Inc.
1409 W Washington
Boise, ID 83702
208-336-5353

Administrator–Division of Vocational Rehabilitation
Len B. Jordon Bldg., Room 150
650 W State
Boise, ID 83720
208-334-3390

Illinois:

Adoption Information Center of Illinois
201 North Wells Street
Chicago, IL 60602
312-346-1516 or 800-572-2390 (in Illinois)

Director of Special Education
Illinois State Board of Education
Mail Code E-216
100 North First Street
Springfield, IL 62777-0001

Director–Protection & Advocacy, Inc.
175 W Jackson, Ste. A-2103
Chicago, IL 60604
312-341-0022 Voice/TDD

Director–Department of Rehabilitation Services
623 E Adams St.
P.O. Box 19429
Springfield, IL 62794-9429
217-785-0218

Coordinating Council for Handicapped Children
20 E Jackson Blvd., Room 900
Chicago, IL 60604
312-939-3513

Designs for Change
220 South State Street, room 1900
Chicago, IL 60604
312-922-0317

Indiana:

Department of Public Welfare
Children and Family Services Division
402 West Washington Street, Room W364
Indianapolis, IN 46204
317-232-5613

Director of Special Education
Division of Special Education
Indiana Department of Education
229 State House
Indianapolis, IN 46204
317-629-9462

Indiana Protection & Advocacy Service Commission
for the Developmentally Disabled
850 N Meridian St., Ste. 2-C
Indianapolis, IN 46204
317-232-1150 or 800-622-4845 (in Indiana)

Commissioner
Indiana Department of Human Services
251 N Illinois St.
P.O. Box 7083
Indianapolis, IN 46207-7083
317-232-7000

Task Force on Education for the Handicapped, Inc.
833 Northside Blvd.
South Bend, IN 46617
219-234-7101

Iowa:

Adoption Program
Department of Human Services
Hoover Building
Des Moines, IA 50319
515-281-5358

Director of Special Education
Division of Special Education
Iowa Department of Public Instruction
Grimes State Office Building
Des Moines, IA 50319-0146
515-281-3176

Director—Iowa Protection & Advocacy Services, Inc.
3015 Merie Hay Rd., Ste. 6
Des Moines, IA 50319
515-281-4311
Iowa Exceptional Parent Center
33 North 12th Street
P.O. Box 1151
Ft. Dodge, IA 50501
515-576-5870

Kansas:

Commission of Adult and Youth Services
Department of Social and Rehabilitation Services
300 SW Oakley
Topeka, KS 66606
913-296-4661

Director of Special Education
Kansas Department of Education
120 E. Tenth Street
Topeka, KS 66612
913-296-4945

Director-Kansas Advocacy & Protection Services
513 Leavenworth, Ste. 2
Manhattan, KS 66502
913-776-1541 or 800-432-8276 (in Kansas)

Commissioner of Rehabilitation Services
Department of Social & Rehabilitative Services
Biddle Bldg., 2nd Floor
2700 W 6th
Topeka, KS 66606
913-296-3911

Families Together, Inc.
P.O. Box 86153
Topeka, KS 66686
913-273-6343

Kentucky:

Cabinet for Human Resources
Department ofr Social Services
275 East Main Street
Frankfort, KY 40621
502-564-2136

Director of Special Education
Kentuckey Department of Education
Office of Education for Exceptional Children
Capitol Plaza Tower, Room 820
Frankfort, KY 40601
501-564-4970

Director–Department of Public Advocacy
Protection & Advocacy Division
1264 Louisville Rd.
Perimeter Park West
Frankfort, KY 40601
502-564-2967 or 800-372-2988 Voice/TDD

Assitant Superintendent of Rehabilitation
Department of Education
Bureau of Rehabilitative Services
Capital Plaza Office Tower
Frankfort, KY 40601
502-564-4440

Kentucky Special Parent Involvement Network
318 W Kentucky Street
Louisville, KY 40203
502-587-5717 or 502-584-1104

Lousiana:

Office of Community Services/Children, Youth and Family
1967 North Street
Baton Rouge, LA 70821
504-342-4086

Director of Special Education
Louisiana Department of Education
Special Education Services
P.O. Box 44064, 9th Floor
Baton Rouge, LA 70804-9064
504-342-3633

Director–Advocate Center for the Elderly & Disabled
1001 Howard Ave., Ste. 300-A
New Orleans, LA 70113
504-522-2337 or 800-662-7705 (in Louisiana)

Director–Division of Rehabilitation Services
P.O. Box 94371
Baton Rouge, LA 70804
504-342-2285

United Cerebral Palsy Center of Greater New Orleans
1500 Edwards Avenue, Ste. O
Harahan, LA 70123
504-733-7736

Maine:

Department of Human Services
221 State Street
Augusta, ME 04333
207-289-5060

Director of Special Education
Division of Special Education
Maine Dept. of Educational & Cultural Services
Station #23
Augusta, ME 04333
207-289-5953

Director–Advocates for the DD
2 Mulliken Court
P.O. Box 5341
Hallowell, ME 04347
207-289-5755 or 800-452-1948 (in Maine)

Director–Bureau of Rehabilitative Services
Department of Health & Welfare
32 Winthrop St.
Augusta, ME 04330
207-289-2266

Special Needs Parent Information Network (SPIN)
P.O. Box 2067
Augusta, ME 04330
207-582-2504 or 800-325-0220 (in Maine)

Maryland:

Family and Children's Services
Social Service Administration
311 West Saratoga Street
Baltimore, MD 21201
301-333-0236 or 800-492-1978

Director of Special Education
Division of Special Education
Maryland State Department of Education
200 W Baltimore Street
Baltimore, MD 21201-2595
301-333-7600

Director–Maryland Disability Law Center
2510 St. Paul St.
Baltimore, MD 21218
301-333-7600

Assistant State Superintendent
Division of Vocational Rehabilitation
State Department of Education
200 W Baltimore St.
Baltimore, MD 21201
301-659-2294

Massachusetts:

Department of Social Services
24 Fannsworth Street
Boston, MA 02110
617-727-0900

Director of Special Education
Division of Special Education
Massachusetts Department of Education
1385 Hancock Street, 3rd Floor
Quincy, MA 02169-5183
617-770-7468

Director–DD Law Center of Massachusetts
11 Beacon Street, Ste. 925
Boston MA 02108
617-723-8455

Commissioner–Massachusetts Rehabilitation Commission
20 Park Plaza, 11th Floor
Boston, MA 02116
617-727-2172

Federation for Children with Special Needs
312 Stuart Street, 2nd Floor
Boston, MA 02116
617-482-2915 or 800-331-0688 (in Massachusetts)

Michigan:

Department of Social Services
P.O. Box 30007
Lansing, MI 48909
517-373-3513

Director of Special Education
Special Education Services
Michigan Department of Education
P.O. Box 30008
Lansing, MI 48909-7508
517-487-1755

Director–Michigan Protective & Advocacy Services, Inc.
109 W Michigan Ave., Ste. 900
Lansing, MI 48933
517-487-1755

Director-Michigan Rehabilitation Services
Michigan Department of Education
P.O. Box 30010
Lansing, MI 48909
517-373-0683

United Cerebral Palsy Association of Metropolitan Detroit
Parents Training Parents Project
17000 West 8 Mile Road, Ste. 380
Southfield, MI 48075
313-557-5070

Citizens Alliance to Uphold Special Education (CAUSE)
313 South Washington Sq., Ste. 040
Lansing, MI 48933
517-485-4084 or 800-221-9105 (in Michigan)

Minnesota:

Department of Human Services
444 Lafayette Road
St. Paul, MN 55155-3831
612-296-0584

Director of Special Education
Special Education Section
Department of Education
812 Capitol Square Building
550 Cedar Street
St. Paul, MN 55101-2233
612-359-3490

Managing Attorney–Legal Aid Society of Minneapolis
222 Grain Exchange Bldg.
323 Fourth Ave., S
Minneapolis, MN 55415
612-332-7301

Assistant Commissioner
Division of Rehabilitation Services
Department of Jobs and Training
390 N Robert St., 5th Floor
St. Paul, MN 55101
612-296-1822

PACER Center, Inc.
4826 Chicago Avenue South
Minneapolis, MN 55417
612-827-2966 or 800-53-PACER (in Minnesota)

Mississipi:

Department of Human Services, Adoption Unit
P.O. Box 352
Jackson, MS 39205
601-354-0341

Director of Special Education
Bureau of Special Services
State Dept. of Education
P.O. Box 771
Jackson, MS 39205-0771
601-359-3498

Director–Mississippi Protection & Advocacy System, Inc.
4793B McWillie Dr.
Jackson, MS 39206
601-981-8207 or 800-772-4057 (in Mississippi)

Director–Department of Rehabilitation Services
Vocational Rehabilitation Division
932 N State Street
P.O. Box 1698
Jackson, MS 39215-1698
601-354-6825

Association of Developmental Organization of Mississippi
6055 Highway 18 South, Ste. A
Jackson, MS 39209
601-922-3210 or 800-231-3721 (in Mississippi)

Missouri:

Division of Family Services
Department of Social Services
P.O. Box 88
Jefferson City, MO 65103
314-751-2882
800-554-2222

Director of Special Education
Department of Elementary and Secondary Education
P.O. Box 480
Jefferson City, MO 65102
314-751-2965

Missouri Protection & Advocacy Services
211-B Metro Drive
Jefferson City, MO 65101
314-893-3333 or 800-392-8667 (in Missouri)

Assistant Commissioner
State Department of Education
Division of Vocational Rehabilitation
2401 E McCarty
Jefferson City, MO 65101
314-751-3251

Missouri Parents Act (MPACT)
P.O. Box 1141 G.S.
Springfield, MO 65808
417-882-7434 or 417-869-6694

Montana:

Department of Family Services
P.O. Box 8005
Helena, MT 59604
406-444-5900

Director of Special Education
Office of Public Instruction
State Capitol, Room 106
Helena, MT 59620
406-444-4429

Director—Montana Advocacy Program
1410 8th Avenue
Helena, MT 59601
406-444-3889 or 800-245-4743 (in Montana)

Administrator—Department of Social & Rehabilitative Services
Rehabilitative-Visual Services Division
P.O. Box 4210
Helena, MT 59604
406-444-2590

Parents, Let's Unite for Kids (PLUK)
1500 N 30th Street
Billings, MT 59101
406-727-4590 or 800-222-PLUK (in Montana)

Nebraska:

Department of Social Services
301 Centennial Mall South
Lincoln, NE 68509
402-471-9331

Director of Special Education
Nebraska Department of Education
P.O. Box 94987
Lincoln, NE 68509-4987
402-471-2471

Director-Nebraska Advocacy Services, Inc.
522 Lincoln Center Building
215 Centennial Mall South
Lincoln, NE 68508
402-474-3183

Associate Commissioner & Director
Division Rehabilitative Services
State Department of Education
301 Centennial Mall, 6th Floor
Lincoln, NE 68509
402-471-2961

Nevada:

Division of Child and Family Services
700 Belrose Street
Las Vegas, NV89158
702-486-5270

Director of Special Education
Nevada Department of Education
Capitol Complex
400 W King street
Carson City, NV 89710-0004

Project Director-Office of Protection & Advocacy
2105 Capurro Way, Ste. B
Reno, NV 89431
702-789-0233 or 800-992-5715 (in Nevada)

Administrator, Rehabilitation Division
Department of Human Resources
Kinkead Bldg., 5th Floor
505 King St.
Carson City, NV 89710
702-885-4440

Nevada Association for the Handicapped
6200 W Oakey Blvd.
Las Vegas, NV 89201-1142
702-870-7050

New Hampshire:

Division for Children and Youth Services
6 Hazen Drive
Concord, NH 03301
603-271-4721

Director of Special Education
New Hampshire Department of Education
101 Pleasant Street
Concord, NH 03301-3860
603-271-3741

Director—Disabilities Rights Center, Inc.
94 Washington St.
P.O. Box 19
Concord, NH 03302-0019
603-228-0432

Director—State Dept. of Education
Division of Vocational Rehabilitation
78 Regional Dr., Bldg. JB
Concord, NH 03301
603-271-3471

Parent Information Center
155 Manchester St.
Concord, NH 03302-1422
603-224-6299

New Jersey:

Division of Youth and Family Services, Adoption Unit
CN 717, 1 South Montgomery Street
Trenton, NJ 08625-0717
609-633-6902

Director of Special Education
Division of Special Education
New Jersey Department of Education
P.O. Box CN 500
225 W State Street
Trenton, NJ 08625-0001
609-292-0147

Director–Division of Advocacy for the Developmentally Disabled
Hughes Justice Complex, CN850
Trenton, NJ 08625
609-292-9742 or 800-792-8600 (in New Jersey)

Director–Division of Vocational Rehabilitation Services
Labor & Industry Bldg., CN398
John Fitch Plaza, Room 1005
Trenton, NJ 08625
609-292-5987

Parents and Children Together Organized for Family Learning (PACTO)
66 Lakeview Drive
P.O. Box 114
Allentown, NJ 08501
201-324-2451

Statewide Parent Advocacy Network (SPAN)
516 North Avenue East
Westfield, NJ 07090
201-654-7726

New Mexico:

Department of Human Services
P.O. Box 2348
Santa Fe, NM 87504
505-827-8423 or 800-432-2075 (in New Mexico)

Director of Special Education
State Department of Education
State Educational Bldg.
Santa Fe, NM 87501-2786
505-827-6541

Protection & Advocacy System
2201 San Pedro, NE
Bldg. 4, Ste. 140
Albuquerque, NM 87110
505-888-0111 or 800-432-4682 (in New Mexico)

Director-Division of Vocational Rehabilitation
604 W San Mateo
Santa Fe, NM 87503
505-827-3511

Education for Indian Children with Special Needs (EPICS)
P.O. Box 788
Bernalillo, NM 87004
505-867-3396

New York:

Department of Social Services, Adoption Services
40 North Pearl Street
Albany, NY 12243
800-345-KIDS

Director of Special Education
New York State Dept. of Education
Office of Education of Children with Handicapping Conditions
Education Building Annex, Room 1073
Albany, NY 12234-0001
518-474-5548

New York Commission on Quality of Care for the Mentally Disabled
99 Washington Ave., Ste. 1002
Albany, NY 12210
518-473-4057

Director-Office of Vocational Rehabilitation
One Commerce Plaza, Room 1907
Albany, NY 12234
518-474-2714

Parent Network Center
1443 Main Street
Buffalo, NY 14209
716-885-1004

North Carolina:

Division of Social Services
325 North Salisbury Street
Raleigh, NC 27603
919-733-3801

Director of Special Education
Division of Exceptional Children
North Carolina State Department of Public Instruction
Education Bldg., Room 442
116 W Edenton
Raleigh, NC 27603-1712
919-733-3921

Director—Govenor's Advocacy Council for Persons with Disabilities
1318 Dale St., Ste. 100
Raleigh, NC 27605
919-733-9250

Director—Division of Vocational Rehabilitation Services
Department of Human Resources, State Office
P.O. Box 26053
Raleigh, NC 27611
919-733-3364

Exceptional Children's Advocacy Council
P.O. Box 16
Davidson, NC 28036
704-892-1321

ARC, North Carolina
Family and Infant Preschool Program
Western Carolina Center
300 Enola Road
Morganton, NC 28655
704-433-2661

North Dakota:

Children and Family Services
Department of Human Services
600 East Boulevard Avenue
Bismarck, ND 58505-0250
701-224-4811

Director of Special Education
Department of Public Instruction
State Capitol
Bismarck, ND 58505-0440
701-224-2277

Director—Protection & Advocacy Project
State Capitol Judicial Wing, 1st Floor
Bismarck, ND 58505
701-224-2972 or 800-472-2670 (in North Dakota)

Director-Division of Vocational Rehabilitation
State Capitol Bldg.
Bismarck, ND 58505
701-224-2907

Pathfinder Services of North Dakota
RRI Box 18-A
Maxbass, ND 58760
701-268-3390

Ohio:

Department of Human Services, Adoptions
65 East State Street
Columbus, OH 43266
800-686-1581 or 614-466-9274

Director of Special Education
Ohio Department of Education
Division of Special Education
933 High Street
Worthington, OH 43085-4017
614-466-2650

Director—Ohio Legal Rights Service
8 E Long St., 6th Floor
Columbus, OH 43215-
614-466-7264 or 800-282-9181

Administrator-Ohio Rehabilitation Services Commission
4656 Heaton Rd.
Columbus, OH 43299
614-438-1210

SOC Information Center
106 Wellington Place, Ste. LL
Cincinnat, OH 45219
513-381-2400

Ohio Coalition for the Education of Handicapped Children
933 High Street, Ste. 106
Worthington, OH 43085
614-431-1307

Oklahoma:

Department of Human Services
P.O. Box 25352
Oklahoma City, OK 73125
405-521-2475

Director of Special Education
State Dept. of Education
Oliver Hodge Memorial Bldg.
2500 N Lincoln, Room 215
Oklahoma City, OK 73105-4599
405-521-3352

Director-Protection & Advocacy Agency
9726 E 42nd Street
Osage Bldg., Ste. 133
Tulsa, OK 74146
918-664-5883

Administrator of Rehabilitation Services
Department of Human Services
23rd & Lincoln, Sequoyah Bldg.
P.O. Box 25352
Oklahoma City, OK 73125
405-521-3646

PRO-Oklahoma (Parents Reaching Out in Oklahoma)
1917 S Harvard Avenue
Oklahoma City, OK 73128
405-681-9710 or 800-PL94-142 (in Oklahoma)

Oregon:

Adoption Services, Children's Services Division
198 Commercial Street SE
Salem, OR 97310
505-378-4121

Director of Special Education
Special Education & Student Services Division
Oregon Department of Education
700 Pringle Pkwy, SE
Salem, OR 97310-0290
503-378-2677

Director–Oregon Developmental Disabilities Advocacy Center
400 Board of Trade Bldg.
310 SW 4th Ave
Portland, OR 97204
503-243-2081

Administrator-Division of Vocational Rehabilitation
Department of Human Resources
2045 Silverton Rd., NE
Salem, OR 97310
503-378-3830

Oregon Coalition for Exceptional Children & Young Adults/COPE
Oregon COPE Project
999 Locust Street, NE, #42
Salem, OR 97303
503-373-7477

Pennsylvania:

Dept. of Public Welfare, Office of Children, Youth and Families
P.O. Box 2675
Harrisburg, PA 17105-2675
717-257-7003

Director of Special Education
Pennsylvania Department of Education
333 Market Street
Harrisburg, PA 17126-0333
717-783-6913

Pennsylvania Protection & Advocacy, Inc.
116 Pine St.
Harrisburg, PA 17101
717-236-8110 or 800-692-7443 (in Pennsylvania)

Director–Office of Vocational Rehabilitation
Labor & Industry Bldg.
Seventh & Forster Streets
Harrisburg, PA 17120
717-787-5244

Parents Union for Public Schools
401 North Broad Street, Room 916
Philadelphia, PA 19108
215-574-0037

Parent Education Network
240 Haymeadow Drive
York, PA 17402
717-845-9722

Rhode Island:

Department for Children & Their Families
610 Mt. Pleasant Avenue
Providence, RI 02908
401-457-4654

Director of Special Education
Rhode Island Department of Education
Roger Williams Bldg., Room 209
Providence, RI 02908-5025
401-277-3505

Director–Rhode Island Protection & Advocacy System
55 Bradford St.
Providence, RI 02903
401-831-3150 Voice/TDD

Administrator-Vocational Rehabilitation Division of Community Services
Department of Human Services
40 Fountain St.
Providence, RI 02903
401-421-70005 or 421-7016 TDD

South Carolina:

Department of Social Services, Division of Adoption & Birth Parent Services
P.O. Box 1520
Columbia, SC 29202
803-734-6095 or 800-922-2504 (in South Carolina)

Director of Special Education
Office of Programs for Handicapped
South Carolina Department of Education
100 Executive Center Drive, A-24
Columbia, SC 29201
803-737-8710

Director—South Carolina Protection & Advocacy System for the Handicapped, Inc.
2360-A Two Notch Road
Columbia, SC 29204

Commissioner—South Carolina Vocational Rehabilitation Department
P.O. Box 15
W Columbia, SC 29171-0015
803-734-4300

South Dakota:

Child Protection Services
Department of Social Services
700 Govenors Drive
Pierre, SD 57501
605-773-3227

Director of Special Education
State of South Dakota Department of Education
Richard F. Kneip Office Bldg.
700 N Illinois St., 3rd Floor
Pierre, SD 57501-2293
605-773-3678

Director–South Dakota Advocacy Project, Inc.
221 S Central Ave.
Pierre, SD 57501
605-224-8294 or 800-742-8108

Division of Rehabilitative Services
Department of Vocational Rehabilitation
State Office Bldg.
700 Govenors Drive
Pierre, SD 57501
605-773-3195

South Dakota Parent Connection
P.O. Box 84813
330 N Main Ave., Ste. 301
Sioux Falls, SD 57118-4813
605-335-8844 or 800-422-6893 (in South Dakota)

Tennessee:

Department of Human Services
400 Deaderick Street
Nashville, TN 37248-9000
615-741-5935

Director of Special Education
State of Tennessee Department of Education
132 Cordell Hull Bldg.
Nashville, TN 37219
615-741-2851

Director–E.A.C.H., Inc.
P.O. Box 121257
Nashville, TN 37212
615-298-1080 or 800-342-1660 (in Tennessee)

Commissioner–Division of Rehabilitation Services
1808 W End Bldg., Room 900
Nashville, TN 37203
615-741-2095

Texas:

Department of Human Services
P.O. Box 149030
Austin, TX 78714-9030
512-45-3302

Director of Special Education
Texas Education Agency
1701 N Congress Ave., Room 5-120
Austin, TX 78701-2486
512-463-9734

Director-Advocacy, Inc.
7700 Chevy Chase Dr., Ste. 300
Austin, TX 78752
512-454-4816 or 800-252-9108 (in Texas)

Texas Rehabilitation Commission
118 E Riverside Drive
Austin, TX 78704
512-445-8100

Partnerships for Assisting Texans with Handicaps (PATH)
6465 Calder Ave., Ste. 202
Beaumont, TX 77707
409-866-4762

Utah:

Division of Family Services
120 North 200 West
Salt Lake City, UT 84103
801-538-4080

Director of Special Education
Utah State Office of Education
250 E. 500 South
Salt Lake City, UT 84111
801-533-5982

Director–Legal Center for the Handicapped
254 W 400 South, Ste. 300
Salt Lake City, UT 84101
801-363-1347 or 800-662-9080 (in Utah)

Director—Vocational Rehabilitation Agency
250 E 500 South
Salt Lake City, UT 84111
801-533-5991

Utah Parent Center
4984 South 300 West
Murray, UT 84107
801-265-9883

Vermont:

Social and Rehabilitation Services
103 South Main Street
Waterbury, VT 05676
802-241-2131

Director of Special Education
Division of Special & Compensatory Education
Vermont Dept. of Education
State Office Bldg.
120 State Street
Montpelier, VT05602-3403
802-838-3141

Director—Vermont DD Protection & Advocacy, Inc.
6 Pine St.
Burlington, VT 05401
802-863-2881

Director—Vocational Rehabilitation Division
Osgood Bldg., Waterbury Complex
103 S Main St.
Waterbury, VT 05676
802-241-2189

Vermont Association for Retarded Citizens
Information and Training Network
37 Champlain Mill
Winooski, VT 05404
802-655-4016

Virginia:

Department of Social Services
Bureau of Child Welfare Services
8007 Discovery Drive
Richmond, VA 23229
804-662-9025 or 800-DO-ADOPT

Director of Special Education
Office of Special & Compensatory Education
P.O. Box 6Q
Richmond, VA 23216-2060

Director–Dept. of Rights for the Disabled
James Monroe Bldg.
101 N 14th St., 17th Floor
Richmond, VA 23219
804-225-2042 or 800-552-3962 (in Virginia)

Department of Rehabilitation Services
Commonwealth of Virginia
P.O. Box 11045
4901 Fitzhugh Ave.
Richmond, VA 23230
804-257-0316

Parent Educational Advocacy Training Center
228 S Pitt St., Ste. 300
Alexandria, VA 22314
703-836-2953 Also serves Maryland and West Virginia

Washington:

Division of Children and Family Services
P.O. Box 45713/ob41
Olympia, WA 98505
206-753-2178

Director of Special Education
Superintendent of Public Instruction
Old Capital Bldg.
Olympia, WA 98502-0001
206-753-6733

Washington Protection & Advocacy System
1550 W Armory Way, Ste. 204
Seattle, WA 98119
206-284-1037 or 800-562-2702 (in Washington)

Director-Division of Vocational Rehabilitation
State Office Bldg., #2
Dept. of Social & Health Services
P.O. Box 1788 (MS 21-C)
Olympia, WA 98504
206-753-0293

Washington PAVE
6316 South 12th South
Tacoma, WA 98645
206-565-2266 Voice/TDD or 800/5-PARENT (in Washington)

West Virginia:

Department of Health and Human Resources
Bureau of Human Resources
Office of Social Services
State Capitol Complex, Bldg. 6
Charleston, WV 25305
304-348-7980

Director of Special Education
West Virginia Department of Education
Bldg., #6, Room B-304
Charleston, WV 25305
304-348-2696

Director-West Virginia Advocates for the Developmentally Disabled, Inc.
1200 Brooks Medical Bldg.
Quarrier St., Suite 27
Charleston, WV 25301
304-346-0847 or 800-642-9205 (in West Virginia)

Director-Division of Rehabilitation Services
West Virginia State Board of Rehabilitation
State Capitol Bldg.
Charleston, WV 25305

Wisonsin:

Department of Health & Social Services
Division of Community Services
P.O. Box 7851
Madison, WI 53707-7851
608-266-0690

Director of Special Education
Division of Handicapped Children & Pupil Services
Department of Public Instruction
125 S Webster
P.O. Box 7841
Madison, WI 53707
608-266-1649

Director-Wisconsin Coalition for Advocacy, Inc.
30 W Mifflin, Ste. 508
Madison, WI 53703
608-251-9600 or 800-328-1110 (in Wisconsin)

Administrator-Division of Vocational Rehabilitation
Department of Health & Social Services
1 Wilson St., Room 850
P.O. Box 7852
Madison, WI 53702
608-266-5466

Parent Education Project
United Cerebral Palsy of SE Wisconsin
230 W Wells Street
Milwaukee, WI 53203
414-272-4500

Wyoming:

Department of Family Services
319 Hathaway Building
2300 Capitol Ave.
Cheyenne, WY 82002
307-777-7561

Director of Special Education
State Department of Education
Hathaway Building
2300 Capitol Ave.
Cheyenne, WY 82002-0050
307-777-7417

Director-Protection & Advocacy System, Inc.
2424 Pioneer Av., #101
Cheyenne, WY 82001
307-632-3496 or 800-624-3496 (in Wyoming)

Administrator-Division of Vocational Rehabilitation
Department of Health & Social Services
326 Hathaway Bldg.
Cheyenne, WY 82002
307-777-7385

GLOSSARY

Understanding Birth Defects

Birth defect is the term used to signify a problem present at birth, such as cleft palate, spina bifida, congenital heart disease, etc. They can also be inherited (genetic), occur as a result of a chromosomal abnormality, or they can result from prenatal complications such as, maternal illness, atypical uterus, drug or alcohol use, or X-ray.

Understanding Genetic Disorders

Autosomal Dominant Disorder is a genetic disorder that a child inherits from a parent who also has the autosomal dominant disorder. "Dominant" refers to the ability of the defective gene to override the normal gene. A child born to a parent who has an autosomal dominant disorder has a 50 percent chance of inheriting the disorder and, if inherited, has a 50 percent chance of passing the disorder on to offspring.

Autosomal Recessive Disorder is a genetic disorder that occurs when a child inherits two defective genes, one from each parent. Either both parents are carriers of the defective gene that causes the disorder, or one parent is a carrier and one parent has the autosomal recessive disorder. "Recessive" means that the defective gene is hidden by the normal gene. When parents are carriers for the same recessive disorder, a child will have a 25 percent chance of having the disorder if each parent's defective gene is inherited. They will have a 50 percent chance of being a carrier if one parent's defective gene and one parent's normal gene are inherited. If both parent's normal genes are inherited, they will have a 25 percent chance that the gene pair will be normal. When one parent has the autosomal recessive disorder and the other parent is a carrier, a child will have a 50 percent chance of being a carrier. If the child inherits only one defective gene, rather than one from each parent, he or she is a carrier and can pass the disorder on to offspring, though they do not have the disorder themselves.

X-Linked Disorders involve genes that are located on the X, also referred to as the female, sex chromosome. Muscular dystrophy and hemophilia fall into the category of X-linked disorders. X-linked disorders can often contribute to some form of intellectual impairment.

Chromosomal Abnormality is the term used to describe a genetic disorder caused by either too many or too few chromosomes, chromosomes with extra or missing

203

pieces, or pieces attached to another chromosome. Down syndrome falls into this category because an extra chromosome 21 is present.

Understanding Developmentally Delayed

Developmental delay refers to the condition of an infant or child who is not achieving new or expected skills in the typical time frame. In addition, he or she may be exhibiting behaviors that are inappropriate for his or her age. Developmental delays may be a result of a specific developmental disability. Other children may be able to catch up to their age appropriate peer group.

Understanding Developmental Disability

Developmental disability is any physical or mental condition with an onset before 18 years of age that causes the child to acquire skills and abilities at a slower rate than his or her peer group. The delays are expected to continue indefinitely, and impair the child's ability to function in society as is expected of his or her same-aged peers. This book focuses primarily on developmental disabilities.

Defining Disease, Disorder, Impairment and Syndrome

Disease is the term used to describe any change or interruption of the normal function or structure of the body, including organs, systems, or parts.

Disorder and *impairment* are interchangeable terms referring to an abnormality or disturbance of normal function, such as a speech disorder.

Syndrome refers to a group of symptoms, signs, or genetic traits which, when occurring together, define a specific disorder or disease.

INDEX